DISCARD

PAGANS IN THE PULPIT

RICHARD S. WHEELER

ARLINGTON HOUSE·PUBLISHERS
NEW ROCHELLE, N. Y.

Library of Congress Cataloging in Publication Data

Wheeler, Richard Shaw, 1935-
   Pagans in the pulpit.

   1. Christianity and politics. 2. Church and social problems. 3. Liberalism (Religion) I. Title.
BR115.P7W44   261.8   74-10903
ISBN 0-87000-264-3

Contents

Preface

Many of the great social enterprises of our times, such as the quest for equality or for peace, have been firmly—even rapturously—supported by the Christian clergy. But somehow, things don't quite fit together. The New Testament, of which I have an extensive knowledge, seems to be saying one thing, while the sermons, tracts, and books of a well-publicized segment of the clergy say something else. Newspapers dwell tenderly on worker-priests, on radical ministers, and on all the currents of theology that seek an opening to the left. In one recent instance a pastor excoriated the Nixon administration for curtailing the poverty program and the Office of Economic Opportunity. He clearly implied that such cutbacks were sinful. He and others like him favor great structural changes in American life: more welfare and social security; more economic equality; public ownership of corporations, or at least rigorous Federal supervision over them; lower-class solidarity; and so on.

The persistence and moral certitude of such a large body of liberal clerics aroused my curiosity. Apparently, they were not only discovering Christian values in secular, left-seeking social doctrine; they were boldly reinterpreting the concept of God Himself, changing him from a personal omniscient Father to a pantheistic abstraction. Moreover, they were seeking the creation of a current Kingdom of Heaven, functioning not so much in the hearts of believers as in perfect social institutions. I worried about all this: perhaps I had missed something great in the faith or had misinterpreted Christianity or had been taught false values. So I began to survey the Scriptures, as well as the various commentaries that illumine them, willing to recast my faith no matter where the inquiry might lead. I would let the historic church speak for itself. It was my obligation to keep an open mind and to modify my beliefs, including my social views, to fit the divine will. I was prepared even to surrender the social conservatism that had been a frame of reference, although not an ideology, through my adult life. So I began a serious, though sometimes intermittent, study of Christian theology, using Catholic, Protestant, and Jewish sources, old and new.

I was particularly mystified by the total absence of institutional reform in the New Testament. It was obvious that neither Jesus nor his apostles were in the least interested in transforming the social structure of their day. The whole thrust of their teaching was toward inner change within individuals, a process that would, of course, ultimately have its effect on institutions. The Gospels begin with John the Baptist's plea for personal repentence and then focus steadily on the rebirth of personality through the Lord. His whole teaching has to do with each man's relationship to God and to his neighbors, friends, strangers, family, and enemies. Christianity teaches a doctrine of personal faith, personal love, personal charity, and personal purity, from which will emanate changes in the way people deal with each other. Jesus was not intent upon discarding the Mosaic law; He preferred to make it work by instilling an eagerness for love and justice in men. The spirit, the *pneuma,* would infuse the creaking legal structure with life. Yet, in our own times, I encountered a clerical obsession with that cold legal structure, with politics and the Congress and the Presidency.

My uneasiness about that strange shift resulted in this book, which examines some contemporary social phenomena in the light of traditional Christian values. The concept of progressive social reform does not exist in the New Testament, either directly or derivatively, even though Christianity is a religion with a unique social ethic. What does exist abundantly is a concern about the condition of the soul. Virtually everything Jesus did was directed toward personal change and reconciliation with God. He encouraged the growth of certain traits of character: love above all, and forgiveness, mercy, charity, patience, and hope and joy, all in the context of a trusting faith. Each of his followers was to become a new person who could discipline his body, love friends and neighbors, care for the widowed and orphaned, and help the diseased and the poor. He began simply with people, with humble building blocks rather than grand social blueprints. He molded the clay of personality and cared little for what legal reforms might achieve. He made it clear that the law was sterile; He had a more fruitful way to transform the world.

There remained, however, a crucial question: Did it follow logically that in modern, complex times the pursuit of institutional change was an extension of Christian love? After the church transformed hearts, was socialism the next step? Contemporary liberal theology leans toward that view and suggests that Christian doctrine compels the faithful to use the lawful processes of benevolent government to assist the distressed—the cant word is "underprivileged." Through such law the poor are to be succored, the unemployed supported, the ill and the blind and the deaf cared for, the rich humbled, the greedy stripped of their lucre, and business run for "social purposes" or "the good of all," whatever that may mean. Theological liberals perceive Christianity as the base for an evolution in legal institutions that will progress toward a socialist utopia. The church is to inspire a desire for reform. Capitalism, private ownership, economic licentiousness, and inequality are all to be wiped out. They are the fruits of sin, and socialism is to demolish them and restore goodness. These reforms are to be imposed from above: by Congress, the executive, the Supreme Court, and the United Nations, all under the moral and ethical guidance of liberal clerics. Evil is to be destroyed and people changed for the better because they will no longer be exploited. Thus, for liberals the linkage between the teachings of Jesus and socialism is natural and inevitable, and the switch from faith to progressive ideology is natural. The social gospel provides an understandable and seductive viewpoint.

Nevertheless, I found the silence of the gospels disturbing. If only Jesus had said *something* prophetic about the evolution of his church toward political reform! If only He had suggested somewhere, *anywhere*, that the transformation of hearts should evolve into a secular politics! The Mosaic law had ordained a system of tithes and the gleaning of fields to support the Levitical class, the priesthood, and the poor, but Jesus proffered no reforms. Indeed, He upheld the system, urging people to be cheerfully generous to God. If only He had advocated income-equalization measures, or denounced the existing military complex, or agitated for lower-class solidarity, or promoted the liberation of Judea from the imperial boot of Rome, or schemed to overthrow the ruling classes! This He failed to do; his silence on such matters was total. That silence makes the entire evolutionary theology of the liberals inferential. To make matters worse, the apostles and church fathers who followed Jesus themselves had nothing to say about political reform. Moreover, Jesus rejected the chance to become a temporal king of the Jews when the opportunity arose. Out of that kingship might have come everything liberals dream of for our own times: wondrous laws regulating business; a marvelous benevolence for the needy and ill; a heavy taxation of the rich, all for the sake of the oppressed; splendid laws governing conditions of employment; an end to the cold war with the Samaritans; the elimination of class and caste; a national crusade to escape Roman imperialism—all with the force and majesty of a divine mind, a code springing from God Himself in the form of perfect Christian socialism. However, Jesus refused to be a temporal king, denouncing satan for offering him worldly power. His apostles did not concern themselves with the social structure of Judea or the political structure of the Roman world. They did not attempt a dual ministry, directed partly toward the reform of institutions and partly toward the salvation of souls. I find their silence devastating, especially so because Rome was in dire need of reform and would have profited from the infusion of virtuous and merciful men into public life. The empire was cosmopolitan: it could easily have accommodated some truculent Jews insisting on a New Deal.

The primitive Christians busied themselves converting all classes, from senators and patricians to slaves and the dispossessed. They did not teach a class solidarity that could be used against the rich, but taught a doctrine of love, faith, and reconciliation—a fraternal concern for others. It was a doctrine based on voluntary endeavor; on gifts of charity rather than welfare based on coercive taxation; on a proffering of love rather than the imposition of law enforced by state violence. In the end, the voluntary Christian method would transform Rome beyond anything that law, imposed on resisting hearts, could achieve.

It was not only the gospels, but all that followed in Acts and the epistles that made me wary of liberal Christianity. From my initial researches emerged the impression that Christianity and socialism shared some goals, but reached them by different means. I was quite wrong, however. The goals of the church conflict sharply with the goals of socialism. Christianity may be concerned about the poor, and it may warn the rich, but it embodies no egalitarian doctrine. Socialism is frankly egalitarian and seeks a vague economic justice that is alien to Christianity. In fact, nothing in traditional Christianity remotely suggests an enforced redistribution of incomes. The denunciation of envy runs as a leitmotiv through the Old and New Testaments. There are also sharp differences in the realm of sexuality, family life, economics, private ownership, the perception of history, the uses of the state, and the very reason for man's existence. The facile liberal theology that seeks a Christian socialism is egregiously wrong, but that is a point developed later in the book and not one that needs elaboration here. What is certain is that St. Paul did not agitate against emperors on behalf of oppressed Christians, or organize sit-ins in the Colosseum, or create a faction in the Roman senate. Ultimately, of course, Christians looked forward to the day when men's social patterns would be modified by the injection of loving, self-disciplined people into the world, but the church was always busy creating such people rather than blueprinting future societies. And so the apostles built brotherhood, founded charities, cared for the poor, the sick, the aged and the widowed, and established churches.

It is a significant comment on their method that they did not assault slavery directly through politics, but conquered it with brotherhood and the golden rule. The church urged Christian masters to be good to their slaves; it urged slaves to be cheerful and obedient to their masters; and it urged both to remember that they were brothers in the Lord. As a result, Christian brotherhood virtually wiped out a deeply rooted ancient institution, not through politics, but with love. It became embarrassing for a Christian master to own a slave who was a brother in Christ. That was how Christianity worked in the world, but the church was always something more than a reforming social force; it was a religion. Its primary task was thus quite different from that of socialism. It sought to reconcile men with God and instill obedience to God. It functioned only partly in the temporal world. It offered a spiritual life that transcended all of socialism's goals. The church dealt with such mysterious things as inner serenity, peace, joy, beauty, ecstacy, virtue, and eternal life. It taught a God who reciprocated love, who sent the Holy Spirit, the Helper, into the world to ease troubles and comfort those in need. It opened up miraculous sources of power and hope. The price for all that was simply faith. Thus, Christianity and socialism pulled in quite opposite directions, or at least in different directions, most of the time. They could not be harnessed as a team.

This is a book about those differences. It is not a rationale for doing nothing: there are numerous Christian means of benevolence, chief of which is church charity. The book is the work of a layman and journalist, seeking answers and not always finding them. My researches did on occasion lead me to abandon previous beliefs, departures that were more often away from socialism than toward it. I made a particular effort to examine ideas and passages that seemed to challenge my views; the result was, not only a total rejection of socialism, but also serious doubt about many aspects of contemporary liberal America, including its carnal entertainments, its governmental invasions of privacy and property, its arrogance, its presumptuous belief that democratic institutions are the salvation of the world, and its intellectual hubris.

In any case, the mixture of religion and politics in this book is explosive. It behooved me to tread as cautiously as I could. I am not a controversialist, and I would rather be quietly persuasive than precipitate an uproar. I am, moreover, a journalist treading in areas that have vexed great and sophisticated theologians whose knowledge of the church and its beliefs is a hundredfold greater than my own. There were times when I thought this labor was reckless, if not audacious, but I have persevered out of a ripening belief that I have a contribution to make. I have written from the standpoint of a Christian centrist, eschewing fundamentalist as well as liberal viewpoints. Although I am a Protestant, I believe Catholics will find the views expressed on these pages compatible with their own. It is my faith and trust that these views embody the core of traditional Christianity.

In the following chapters I discuss five diverse contemporary political and social phenomena: the peace movement, the political exploitation of suffering, rebelliousness toward good authority and government, women's liberation, and the egalitarian obsession of democracy. Common to all these discussions is a search for scriptural guidelines that may validate or disqualify these trends. It is an effort to let the New Testament illumine the goals as well as the paths taken by these social enterprises.

There is an amazing phenomenon discernible in each of these issues: Christianity is arrayed not against amoralists, except on questions of sexuality, but against supermoralists who find the teaching of Jesus inadequate. It is the incredible irony of our times that the church is forced to the defensive and must confront persons whose zeal for immediate paradise induces them to reject the counsels of God. The church, always the cornerstone that the powerful builders reject, confronts people who insist on material equality, on an omnipotent peacekeeping mechanism, on the divine right of anarchy, on a government whose function is perfect benevolence, and on the abolition of sex roles. In all instances the teachings of the church have been consciously or unconsciously set aside in favor of secular absolutes. Secular men have concluded that the church is an archaic relic, espousing primitive semitic tribal values unfit for mass democracy. The tragedy of such secular supermoralizing is that it is utterly impossible, and the more men strive to achieve it, the worse will be their despair and guilt. Christians trust in a perfectly good God rather than a perfectly good world and depend on a sublime concept, redemption through the cross, to bring a workable morality into the world of weak-willed and foolish men.

This book is not particularly concerned with church history, but rather with doctrine. At first blush, Christian doctrine seems to have precious little to do with society: it is difficult to discern any vital link between this exegesis and the material world with its traffic jams, smog, aerospace layoffs, railroad bankruptcies, and professional football games. One might well ask what possible difference it makes whether socialism and Christianity are compatible. The world roars along quite well on its own trajectory: the methods of science will soon lead man toward total dominion over his universe. He is coming ever closer to harnessing all the forces of nature, even including the genetic factors that govern the creation of his own flesh. He is even beginning to understand the chemical and electronic factors that govern his thought and logic. In such a modern milieu the ancient doctrine of Christianity seems irrelevant.

In fact, however, it is more relevant than ever. Science is devoid of the means to evaluate itself or to impose a moral system upon its own works. Technology marches ahead without regard to good or evil or man's ultimate purpose. It produces penicillin as well as nuclear bombs, life-saving drugs as well as death-dealing weapons. Science must produce both: it cannot create only one and leave the other realm blank. Thus, science has given man ever-increasing dominion over his life and the forces of nature, but has not supplied him with even an inkling of what to do with his newfound power. The empiric authority of science melts away when it confronts the ultimate moral questions. The metes and bounds of God's law thus acquire crucial importance as we enter an era in which a lack of moral or ethical understanding could lead to the doom of our species and most other life.

I do not simply adduce an argument for the relevance of Christian faith and doctrine in these times; rather, I posit it as a necessity. Without God's transcendent authority we are adrift amid terrible shoals and unable to resolve the dilemmas of power that science imposes on us. Christianity is a revealed religion resting on faith and thus wholly different from the empiric knowledge deployed by science. We are at a point of history where we are discovering that we cannot survive without that revealed authority of God. If we are, as the behaviorist psychologists insist, merely elaborate machines, a mass of ganglions and chemicals reacting and reflexing to impersonal environmental pressures, then we have no particular reason not to bomb each other. However, if we are not a biological accident, then we may confidently walk through the valley of the shadow of death and fear no evil. This is a book about the direction we must take while we are in that valley.

PAGANS
IN THE
PULPIT

1
The Politics
of Suffering

I

Most liberal politics are directed ultimately toward the relief of real or imagined suffering. It is difficult, if not impossible, for a democratic politician of any party to inform his constituents that they must be willing to suffer for a time if they wish to achieve long-term gains. In a democracy, there is no way that politicians can even admit that suffering has positive effects on the growth of character or that benign neglect of some types of suffering can result in a more mature and fruitful resolution of a problem than political intervention can achieve. No upright, franchised, equalized elector wants to hear such nonsense, and he is likely to switch his allegiance to whomever has an instant solution in his hip pocket for almost any problem. Presidents and governors and congressmen are forced to make a show of solving things even when wisdom suggests doing nothing. Only a regime somewhat removed from popular passions and cupidities can dare to ignore for even a moment any form of suffering, even for a good reason. In a profound national emergency a democratic leader may request sacrifice, or a degree of suffering, from his people, but even then it is risky. Winston Churchill asked Britons to suffer, and they promptly ejected him at the end of the war.

Even while the electorates of the western democracies demand increasing services from governments and elect politicians with programs, there is nonetheless a mounting cynicism observable in Europe and the United States about the efficacy of more welfare, or nationalization, or regulation—or even taxes. The two seem to go hand in hand: the greater the demand for public solutions, the deeper the cynicism about them. While most citizens are well aware of the vast range of services proffered by the welfare states, they are equally aware that their personal happiness does not increase. In fact, if anything, there is more melancholia and frustration and despair on every hand than ever, even while the politicians feverishly implement new programs. Private suffering flourishes, often as the very fruit of bureaucratic blundering. Nevertheless, the

15

electorates almost ritualistically support the "progressives" who never talk about the growth of human character amid tribulation, but only about the bliss of having no cares.

Most of us are aware that very little state enterprise affects our lives directly. It always seems to be aimed at those others we call pressure groups or "interests." When we are young, we read about Social Security benefits being raised for the retired; when we are old, we read about mortgage subsidies for young families. Our daily burdens remain very much with us, regardless of who is in Washington or the state house or whether the state benevolence flows toward liberal hangers-on or conservative clients.

Most of our suffering lies beyond the purview of the state. What is government to do about a widow's sudden grief? Or about the agony of lacking the intelligence or good character we need for a career we cherish? Or about an alcoholic spouse? Or about the onset of leukemia in the child we adore? We submit to our little triumphs and tragedies, scarcely aware of the state and its proliferating agencies, even those agencies established to wipe out leukemia, alcoholism, or joblessness. And when the state does finally impinge, usually around April 15 of each year, or when we are ticketed for running a stop sign, or when the state fails to protect our property and persons from rioters, we see the government only as an instrument of additional suffering.

The obsequious politicians nonetheless peddle nostrums that, under other circumstances, would evoke the wrath of the Food and Drug Administration. Is leukemia incurable? Then they stand in line to vote more research funds. Is a widow's grief inconsolable? Then they rush to raise death benefits. Suffering is the mother's milk of politics. The supply is endless and so is the pharmacopoeia in the politicians' kit bags. They have at hand the greatest resources of society: the power to tax and the power to legislate. With these great engines of benevolence they seek in all sincerity to bottle up the world's grief.

Most politicians mean well and hope that they can ease the predicaments of their society, but they are also aware that compassion is a marketable political commodity on election day. There are few among them willing to admit publicly that suffering is a valid aspect of the human experience and crucial to human maturity. The few statesmen among them who know that suffering plays a positive role in the evolution of a virtuous and industrious citizenry or that there are social and political values beyond the immediate relief of pain rarely are free to express such views. Only a great leader such as Winston Churchill was able to do so at the appropriate time, offering the prospect of blood, sweat, and tears in order to preserve the very constitution of his nation.

Britons responded to him through the war. They suffered privation upon privation: death, austerity, cold, pain, exhaustion, grief, dislocation, fear, and conscription as the lamps of liberty were temporarily extinguished. They suffered cruelly, but willingly, because a courageous leader described suffering as a means to a great end. It was not in vain. England survived; its liberties were restored. The island kingdom, seat of empire, cradle of much of the world's genius, master of world commerce, the sceptered isle, the domain of His Britannic

Majesty survived to live, if not to grow, thanks to the moral courage of a man who understood what suffering could achieve.

It is a maxim of democratic politics always to be arrayed against suffering and sacrifice and to blame the opposition for all of it that exists in the world. John Kennedy's famous aphorism—ask not what your country can do for you, but what you can do for your country—came close to being an exception, hence a notable phrase, but the circumstance was wrong. It was duly understood as noble rhetoric and then quietly buried in the rush to deluge Democratic Party client groups with fat parcels of the New Frontier. Mr. Nixon plays the same game. And so Mr. Kennedy's moment was lost, and politics dissolved back to normalcy. Perhaps that was to be expected. One is generally not called upon to suffer, to sacrifice, and to give except in darkening crises, when war clouds hover or when revolution and disruption threaten.

Great social and religious enterprises frequently warn their adherents that they will face persecution and suffering, although the concept is rarely found in politics itself. For the Christian, the necessity to carry one's cross is always at hand. The major ideologies also warn of burdens. For Christians, however, these ordeals are a part of the sacrifice joyously offered to advance the kingdom of heaven, which is not a utopian goal, but allegiance to God. The Communists, too, have always offered their cadres the prospect of persecution, all for their utopian vision of the coming worker's paradise. That dream of paradise is believable to some, even as the cross lives for Christians, and these transcendent understandings create a willingness to endure the most terrible sorrows imaginable for something greater.

But it is usually among fanatics that a willingness to sacrifice or suffer in the present goes hand in hand with a vision of a happy social order in the future. It is at the fanatic extremes of politics and ideology that citizens congregate, fully believing that the triumph of their social ideology will somehow relieve their personal suffering. There are libertarians who are persuaded that, if only the state were sliced down to a small fraction of its current size, they would be miraculously freed in their daily lives. And there are socialists who are convinced that, if only all private business were taken over and run by the government for the common weal, their personal happiness would blossom and flourish. The very thing that binds most men to moderation, to a status quo politics, is a native skepticism about that prospect. Undergirding the views of most centrists and moderates is the understanding that no reform or ideology or majority will ultimately free them or transform their private lives or alter their daily suffering. It is not that moderate men reject all reforms and programs, but rather that they are not sanguine about the effects. When they vote for progressives, it is more from a sense of good citizenship than in any belief that progressive programs will alleviate their personal sorrows.

One of the curiosities of our politics is the diligence with which officeholders try to overcome that skepticism. One recollects the cadences of Great Society rhetoric, the breathtaking promises that suffering shall cease forthwith, that poverty shall be abolished, and that the Moses in the White House will lead the people straight through the Red Sea to the promised land. Mr. Nixon is more

17

subdued, but he succumbs to the temptations nonetheless, proclaiming peace in our time. However, memory serves well: each of us remembers his private griefs and agonies, the tears, losses, frustrations, pain, defeats; we remember these things deep in our hearts and without any recollection of who were the incumbents at the time.

II

The varieties of suffering are as numerous as those who are burdened. Who has not wondered whether any one else could understand the demons and wounds he lives with every hour? We try to bridge the chasm with words and fail. Suffering is too personal. We cannot give voice to our hurt. We can only dimly understand the pain of others, however we sympathize. Some of the things that wound us terribly leave others untouched. One of us is desperately lonely; another rejoices in being alone. Our particular burdens, woven from the strands of our lives, are as unique as fingerprints, and that is why we so frequently misunderstand each other's agonies and needs.

There are several types of suffering that can be readily categorized. Some suffering, such as childbirth, is episodic, while other suffering, such as blindness, is chronic. Chronic suffering necessitates constant aid or subsidy or special care, while episodic suffering is best dealt with through short-range help or insurance. We insure against collision or fire or theft, but we subsidize the blind, the widows of war, and the permanently disabled.

Episodic suffering can be perceived as an ordeal that heals or passes: divorce, loss of a job, social rejection, a humiliation, losses from floods or wind or lightning, loss of a beloved one, or being drafted. Chronic suffering, on the other hand, runs deeper and persists through life. It includes such things as madness, poverty, loneliness, depression, imprisonment, self-hatred, blindness, deafness, loss of limbs, impotence, shyness, imbecility, genius, lack of self-discipline, alcoholism, being orphaned, addiction, fear, mania, racial discrimination, the desperate need for love, guilt, hatred, wasting disease, and unforgiveness. Chronic suffering is deeper and more aggravating because remedies are fewer and hope less possible. Who can replace vision, or heal a mad psyche? We do what we can with painkillers, mood-changing drugs, diversions, and pittances, but those who suffer chronic grief usually suffer alone, without hope, even when surrounded by all the good will in the world.

Suffering can also be categorized into that which afflicts the mind and that which afflicts the body. Physical suffering is almost universal and reaches into virtually every life at some time or another, even though we live in an era of anesthetics. Emotional and mental suffering is universal: no one escapes it, although many can grow from it. Much physical suffering is episodic: broken bones, operations, curable disease, fever, and injuries from accidents. These take their toll, but in time heal and disappear. By contrast, other physical afflictions are permanent or terminal: loss of limbs or organs, disfigurement, uncontrollable cancer, arthritis, addiction, birth defects, a humped back or polio-stricken leg. Sheer weakness, the disabilities of age, emphysema, and syphilis—

18

all have caused untold suffering, shame, and helpless rage.

We suffer, too, the gamut of diseases of the soul and mind. Our emotions storm within us, and the hurts, though not physical, are as real and powerful as anything we endure. Madness, neurosis, depression, psychosis, delusions, loss of self-esteem, frustration, loneliness, hunger for death, fear, violent hatreds—all are terrible agonies of the spirit. We are all aware of the sufferings of our souls: we have each experienced a moment or more of madness, a time of grief, an unbearable emotion. Anxiety, the disease that is endemic among modern men, generates its own quota of suffering. We feel helpless and we feel afraid, and together these yoked problems ulcerate our stomachs and torment our hearts and plunge us into terrible insomnias. If ever there were a perfect devil's tool, it would be anxiety. It wears us down, abrades our souls, and exhausts our strength until our only comfort and hope is the oblivion of sleep.

We must distinguish, too, between circumstantial suffering, which befalls us without our consent, and the suffering we elect or accept as being worthwhile. The circumstances that evoke suffering are infinite: war, weather, revolution, crop failure, plagues, police states, taxes, tortures, our biological inheritance, race, environmental influence, and strikes. We choose none of these things. We do not choose to be orphaned. We do not choose to be black or deaf or paranoid. We do not choose to live in Moscow or be incarcerated at Auschwitz. We do not choose to be shot at in Dallas or Baltimore or Los Angeles. These things come upon us, savage us, and inflict turmoil and terror on us.

On the other hand, we often choose to suffer with the hope that our sacrifice will produce good for ourselves and others. Athletes and volunteer soldiers suffer for victory. I suffer the pains of creativity for the sake of rewards. Spies suffer anonymity and the risk of death for the sake of their nations and their ideologies. Particularly, we suffer for our ideals. The soldier suffers for democracy or, for that matter, for the proletariat or the Führer. We suffer for our faith in our Lord. Nowhere is there a more vivid picture of this than in St. Paul's description of spiritual Jews, recorded in his letter to the Hebrews. These were men, says Paul,

> who through faith conquered kingdoms, enforced justice, received promises, stopped the mouths of lions, quenched raging fire, escaped the edge of the sword, won strength out of weakness, became mighty in war, put foreign armies to flight. Women received their dead by resurrection. Some were tortured, refusing to accept release, that they might rise again to a better life. Others suffered mocking and scourging, and even chains and imprisonment. They were stoned, they were sawn in two, they were killed with the sword; they went about in skins of sheep and goats, destitute, afflicted, ill-treated—of whom the world was not worthy—wandering over deserts and mountains, and in dens and caves of the earth.

What a testament that is to the power of men to suffer gladly for the sake of their religion, for a thing infinitely larger than themselves.

One type of suffering that deserves special mention is the suffering induced by the state. It is the only human institution with a monopoly on coercion and the power to confiscate wealth. Thus, the potential for abuse—for causing suffering—is infinite unless the chains of a constitution are strong and binding. The sufferings caused by state regimes are the very hallmarks of the 20th century. There have been persecutions, not only of the Jews and kulaks, but of Christians, various African tribes, Indians, and Chinese peasants. States banish people, dislocate families, abolish rights, confiscate wealth, impose unbearable taxes, imprison dissidents, abolish religion, torture minorities, harass businessmen, spy on citizens, ostracize the unwanted, conduct bloody wars, permit armies to pillage, mock justice, deny fair trials, separate loved ones, compel austerity, limit one's choice of consumer goods, obscure the news, deny facts, and twist truth. People endure more evils at the hands of rulers than from any other source, and thus no catalogue of suffering is complete without due mention of the dark works of even the most benevolent states.

Yet another genre of suffering can be described as philosophic. There are those among us whose mental anguish derives from their assessment of events. This vicarious suffering is as deep and real as a disease, even if it resides only in the soul. Philosophers are sad. A pessimism about man and his evils can lead quickly to despair and even to suicide. Agnosticism, that suspension of all hope in Divine Love, is a source of such suffering. So is an obsession with war or with malevolent technologies or with nuclear oblivion. This suffering is the special curse of academics, and it is a grief almost palpable in their cloistered halls and libraries.

There is one more type of suffering that includes all the others, but goes beyond them all. I refer to those tortures that can be described only as diabolic or demonic; the works of ghouls. Not, mind you, the work of some comic spirit in red longjohns, sporting a spade beard and horns, but rather the palpable force of evil that rejoices in evil itself and whose fruits are misery. One thinks of those diabolists who made lampshades of human skin at the concentration camps and those angels of hell, in black leather jackets, who sadistically pulverized a helpless victim with tire chains, burning cigarettes, and other means of torture. No matter whether you conceive of satan as a real spirit, a veritable fallen angel, or whether you accept the idea of such evil as myth or metaphor, you nonetheless confront such pulsating evil frequently in the course of life. One thinks of the opium traffic and the pornography trade as demonic. The sufferings of the slaves of opium are beyond description, and the tortures of lust take a cruel toll of a man's character and strength. Such sufferings are everywhere: they are often the work of self-proclaimed witches, or diabolists.

This catalogue, then, covers most species of torment, although others exist. Suffering is the quality of enduring pain and anguish, and it is present in every facet of life. Tragically, we permit ourselves to suffer a great deal for no good reason. I think of the teenager who tortures himself with the fear of being unpopular, even though in due time he will come to realize that popularity is ephemeral and unimportant. We suffer because we think we are not beautiful or because we think we are dull or clumsy, and only rarely do we dismiss these false objectives as unimportant and not worth the pain. Nonetheless, the suffering is real to the sufferer. Is the child who awakens at night screaming from a nightmare any less of a sufferer because he fantasized his terror? I think not. He suffered as truly as one suffers with a headache or from unemployment.

Much of our suffering is relative. It relates to our hopes and our needs, as we conceive them to be. An ascetic hermit, for example, might be perfectly at home in a log cabin without plumbing, while at the same time a suburban housewife might be tormented by such raw circumstance. Suffering depends in part on what we expect from life; the more we expect, the greater is the chance that we will endure great pain while reaching our goals. The problem of expectation will bulk large in our examination of the impact of suffering on public affairs. Those who formulate our hopes for us—preachers, politicians, advertising copywriters, educators, parents—often induce suffering by creating a tension between what is and what we are urged to hunger for. Much of what goes under the banner of liberal politics is an effort to create certain hungers, certain suffering based on rising hopes. The common denominator to all our varied suffering is that the pain is real to ourselves. If we experience no pain, we are not suffering. One wonders whether the avoidance of pain is a very good basis for a national politics.

III

To suffer is to endure. One endures not only the crises, but the long, painful aftermaths. This quality of endurance has received scant attention because it lacks drama. There is a great literature about crises and their impact on our private and public lives, but very little about humble endurance, which fosters such plain virtues as patience and forbearance. Of course, not all suffering involves long-term endurance, but much does. One thinks of the Russian peasants enduring the yoke of the Kremlin with resignation and little hope of improvement. The forces that govern their lives are beyond reform. Or one thinks of the Cubans enduring Castro or the Rumanian Christians persecuted by an atheist regime. All of it is unspectacular and unsung, yet terribly real to those who must endure through the months and years.

It is a psychological commonplace that crisis alters character. One is plunged into the vortex of catastrophe and one emerges, in time, either stronger or weaker, but rarely the same. Some of us gain strength in such circumstance. We discover inner resources that enable us to carry on with new confidence and courage. For others, however, crisis leads to defeat, loss of self-esteem, and a shriveling of the soul. The long-term endurance we associate with suffering has less spectacular results. Patience leads to more patience, and endurance enhances the ability to endure.

There is this quality about suffering: even while it gradually builds our private ability to cope, it has the effect of grinding us down so that our spirits sag, our hearts sink, our souls cry out in anguish, and we reach the bitter conclusion that we are alone. One scarcely finds a joyous sufferer, except among the saints, who learned to thank God for all things, even those that tormented them worst. Perhaps those saints took the long view and perceived suffering as a cool crucible that slowly altered their very natures by purging the dross. We are not all saints, however, and not one man in a hundred accepts his suffering with such philosophy. For most of us, suffering is an agony, and agony is the fruit of things gone wrong. And when things go awry, men seek aid from the state, the one institution with the puissance to help. This opens the possibility that government ultimately weakens its citizens if it becomes too zealous to relieve them of their ordeals. Is it possible that a humane politics bears within it the seeds of disaster or leads inexorably to the decline of nations and civilizations? It is a question I cannot answer.

Suffering can stupify and erode a good heart as well as strengthen one. There comes a time when we suffer too much, when the will collapses and hope dies. What then? Is the state to ignore a desperate man's ordeal? Did Stalin help the kulaks by starving them to death? Are all the resources of charity and mercy to be stilled by the proposition that such a helping hand would deny a man a chance to grow? I think of blacks, oppressed and stupefied by the accumulation of too many hurts, too many insults to the spirit and the will. Who is to say that it is better for them to suffer? There is no doubt that we can grow from our ordeals or that, in Christian terminology, God can make all things work for the best. That cannot, of course, rationalize the cold shoulder, the stony heart, and the merciless mind. As far as possible, sufferers must be helped, if not by the state, then privately, with our bare hands, our charities, our simple friendships and concern.

We can endure our suffering in various ways. Perhaps the simplest is patience, which stands beside hope as the way we bind our wounds. Much suffering involves forces about which we can do nothing. We are helpless to bring a loved one back to life or sew back a lost limb or prevent a child's unhappy marriage. We cannot free prisoners of war of our own accord, nor stand athwart a revolution and stop it. Much suffering is even beyond hope, for what hope has the blind man or the lifer in prison or the basket case in the VA hospital? Whatever hope they muster must spring from some substitution. Thus, the lifer may discover his freedom in God; the blind man may discover new sight in music; the basket case may walk in poetry.

The Christian has, in addition to patience and hope, the resource of faith, from which can leap not only a rocklike steadiness, but even an insouciant joy and a rich hope in the future. His faith rests on the proposition of God, and it derives meaning and progress from everything, good and bad, that happens to him. From merely the human perspective, who is to say whether a calamity is all evil? From God's perspective, these shipwrecks may have served to sink conceits or intolerance or to bury an impossible past. We all hear stories in which a man's disaster proves to be the turning point in his life. Was the disaster therefore good? Not in itself, perhaps, but surely in its effects. Thus, the Christian finds himself assured. A litany of hope and assurance runs melodically through the entire Bible. In its pages a Christian learns that God will never abandon him, even in dungeons and concentration camps. He learns also that God will not tempt him beyond what he can endure and that He will make all things work for the good, even though things often seem hopelessly bad. Therefore, a Christian should give thanks for all things, even the most grievous,

22

because that is God's command. St. Paul put it all together this way: " . . . so we rejoice in our sufferings, knowing that suffering produces endurance, and endurance produces character, and character produces hope, and hope does not disappoint us because God's love has been poured into our hearts through the Holy Spirit which has been given to us." (Rom. 5:3)

Christianity, however, promises much more to those who believe than merely the growth of their character and the gift of hope. It also promises mercy. Jesus spent a large part of his ministry healing those who were diseased in body and spirit. He promised that his Spirit would continue to heal and comfort future generations. He promised that his yoke would be easy. Long before Jesus, the psalmists described God as a mighty refuge, a fortress, a haven from fear and cruelty. The faithful have discovered the unending truth of those promises and have thus learned to bear their sufferings with the special courage of men who are close to God. It is rare that a faithful man feels abandoned.

Although we have dealt with the hope Christians feel when coping with their private suffering, there is much more. Christianity is a great enterprise that inspires in its congregations a willingness to suffer incredible torments in the name of the Lord. Jesus warned that there would be persecution, which did occur through all the succeeding epochs. For the persecuted he promised a special reward: God would heap honors on those who endured for His sake. Many have suffered gladly for their Lord and have found themselves both edified by their sacrifice and greatly revered. Further, they discovered that their own sufferings disappeared and merged into the larger sufferings for their sacred faith. Indeed, suffering for the church became a matter of joy, of boasting, of exhilaration. Listen to St. Paul proclaim his triumph:

> But whatever anyone dares boast of—I am speaking as a fool—I also dare to boast of that. Are they Hebrews? So am I. Are they Israelites? So am I. Are they descendants of Abraham? So am I. Are they servants of Christ? I am a better one—I am talking like a madman—with far greater labors, far more imprisonments, with countless beatings, and often near death. Five times have I received at the hands of the Jews the forty lashes less one. Three times I have been beaten with rods; once I was stoned. Three times I have been shipwrecked; a night and a day have I been adrift at sea; on frequent journeys, in danger from rivers, danger from robbers, danger from my own people, danger from Gentiles, danger in the city, danger in the wilderness, danger at sea, danger from false brethren; in toil and hardship, through many a sleepless night, in hunger and thirst, often without food, in cold and exposure . . .

One marvels that Paul should boast of all this! One can scarcely imagine such a willingness to endure appalling suffering unless the vision that impelled him was majestic and powerful and beautiful beyond description. Yet it is a testament to the faith that many do suffer such things for it, that so many willingly lay down every comfort they possess to serve this towering vision of a redeemed mankind. In the West, in what was once called Christendom before secularization set in, this cast of mind was common. Men gave themselves gladly to further the faith and to serve their transcendent God. They often gave the same devotion to secular causes, both good and bad, with sometimes bloody and fanatical results. Thus, Christendom inculcated a character that was willing to endure great sacrifice for a higher cause. The very civilization that nourished an untrammeled individualism also nourished an eagerness to serve and suffer for princes and popes.

One finds the ghost of that sort of commitment today in the obsessed ideologues. George McGovern had his True Believers, and so did George Wallace. The young, in particular, saw something chiliastic in McGovern, and they flocked to him with a fanaticism that evoked an echo of religious conviction. Their sufferings on behalf of McGovern were pale, of course, compared to those of Paul. In fact, they seemed to inflict more suffering than was inflicted on them when they overturned Chicago in 1968 or spit themselves dry at the 1972 delegates in Miami Beach. Even so, their secular religion was enough to spur them to frenetic action and to evoke a great peyote-bean vision of the reign of St. George. Like so many Christians, some of them found surcease from their personal torments by joining actively in the hopes and sufferings of the McGovern religion. They were a children's crusade: they suffered even the ultimate ignominy of shorn hair that they might appear square enough to attract middle America.

Thus is suffering often endured for great enterprises. Ask any historian of the labor movement. Ask any child of the pioneers. Ask any Mormon. Suffering cannot be perceived merely as an evil in the world or the province of masochists, especially when people so frequently profit from it or achieve new spirituality therefrom or aid their fellows through it. Nor can it be said that suffering bears no fruit. The whole Christian experience militates against that notion. Suffering has value, which raises the uneasy question of what governments should do about it. The politicians have the immediate answer: get rid of it. Abolish pain and deprivation. War on poverty, war on disease, war on depravity. If only it were that simple. Instead, the longer one ponders, the more one is led to expect that governments can scarcely alter the sum total of suffering; they can only rearrange it, reorder it. And one suspects, even more darkly, that the quest to abolish pain—that is, the quest to abolish the curse of Adam—must result in a condition all the more terrible if the state attempts the task. On the other hand, perhaps such a view is much too pessimistic. At any rate, it is time to examine the politics of suffering and see what governments can and what they cannot do with decency to relieve our hurts.

IV

The politics of suffering is primarily the politics of liberals. It is also the hallmark of secular intellectuals and politicians, and it forms the badge of humanitarianism that liberals like to claim as their exclusive property. The clientele of the liberal politician are those perceived to be suffering the most and suffering in a chronic sense rather than infrequently; at least, that is how these clients view themselves, no doubt aided by the alarums of the secular press. Such clients have traditionally included the very poor, the dispossessed, the colored, the forces of labor, the ethnics (still sojourners in a strange land), the suffering Jews, the intellectuals (who persist in the belief they are lonely voices crying in the wilderness), the educators, and the very rich, whose suffering consists in a petrifying guilt about their status. All of these, and more, have formed the special interests, the coalitions of liberalism. In addition, liberals have sought to add the aged, the feminists, and the youth vote to their coalition, and with some success. Except for the very rich, whose participation is a form of masochism, these groups share the feeling that they are the exploited, the suffering outsiders, the kids in the cold with their nose pressed to the glass. They are mostly Democrats.

The politics of conservatism is more sanguine about suffering. It assumes that the endurance of great pain is not limited to the impoverished or alien classes, but is universal and is a part of the human condition. The middle class suffers in its own way, and so do the rich and the Daughters of the American Revolution. This broader concept of suffering does not evoke a callousness toward the poor and dispossessed, but rather a caution about transferring wealth and power from one group to another merely to equalize misery. The argument is much the same as Shylock's:

> I am a Jew. Hath not a Jew eyes? hath not a Jew hands, organs, dimensions, senses, affections, passions? fed with the same food, hurt with the same weapons, subject to the same diseases, healed by the same means, warmed and cooled by the same winter and summer as a Christian is? If you prick us do we not bleed? if you tickle us do we not laugh? if you poison us do we not die? and if you wrong us shall we not revenge? if we are like you in the rest, we will resemble you in that.

Shylock argues from the standpoint of universal humanity, from the universality of suffering. A conservative politics assumes much the same thing. This leads to a skepticism about the virtue of forcibly redistributing income from rich to poor and to an equal skepticism about burdening the state with numerous programs to assist such special interests as the liberal client groups. Add to this the conservative suspicion that the taxes and ordinances of the state are often more burdensome than helpful, and the result is a philosophy of negative government: that which governs best governs least. Beyond that, conservative politics is deeply infused with Christian values; hence it readily perceives the religious and charitable alternatives for sufferers, and it understands the occasional benefit that is to be derived from benign neglect of those in distress. In conservatism, the hope for relief of the poor and unfortunate is diffused widely in charity, insurance, religion, capitalism, and laissez-faire economics, as well as in the state directly. Liberal politics, on the other hand, centers on the state exclusively. Its hope lies in the cloistered precinct of socialism, undiluted by untidy liberty.

It is this perception of widespread suffering that inspires conservatives to dampen the class wars fomented on the left. That even the very rich suffer cruelly is a proposition scarcely admitted in some quarters. Consider with compassion, for example, the plight of Howard Hughes, who for decades has been a prisoner of his wealth. His untold millions of dollars have denied him the freedom enjoyed by even the humblest of men. He can neither go for a Sunday drive in the country, nor visit a favorite hamburger stand, nor invite guests to his home. He is denied access to a church. His eye is never treated to new sights, and his senses are denied new adventures. His is perhaps an extreme case, but nevertheless a valid example of the universality of suffering.

From the left, this conservative awareness of widespread suffering is taken for callousness toward the poor or as corrupt allegiance to such moneyed classes as the steel barons or the lumber moguls or the oilmen. Corporations, after all, cannot suffer. They are the legal creatures of the rich, and they exploit the dispossessed. And so the myth persists that a conservative politics is a creature of the powerful. Any resistance to the liberal politics of suffering is perceived as a coldness to the humble and needy. Such is not the case, however, as long as conservative politicians seek to open private channels of mercy while closing public means; not while they are motivated by a dread of Leviathan and a love of liberty; not so long as earnest conservatives believe and demonstrate that their programs are aimed at the very roots of suffering.

In recent years liberals have discovered that their programs have failed, and failed badly. It was once their fond hope, for example, to abolish the suffering in the slums by installing the sufferers in new government-built homes. After all, was not that suffering caused by the rotten environment of the slums? Unfortunately, things worked out differently. The slum dwellers simply turned their new homes into new slums, to the point where many are now abandoned, gaunt skeletons of a liberal vision, and the slum sufferers still suffer. More recently, the entire Great Society has been found wanting. The poverty program has been chastised for its impotence—and this by the very authors of the program. Suffering persists as much as ever, in familiar ways and new. These discoveries are traumatizing the liberal soul. There are some who take the failures as a sign that the programs were not extensive enough, but others on the left question the validity of the American type of socialism and welfare.

If the apparent failure has dynamited the idealism that inspired these social enterprises, however, it has also exposed the naked greed of the client groups. Despite the lack of results, the pressures continue to maintain every program, frequently on the realistic ground that to abolish them would only produce more suffering. While such suffering might well be the sudden unemployment of a poverty bureaucrat instead of a new burden on the poor, it would nonetheless be suffering. Thus, the nation is saddled with an array of costly malfunctioning programs whose total impact on suffering is inconsequential. Not much can be done until the client groups themselves find the courage to examine the impact of such largesse on their own self-esteem and pride and courage.

The importunities of the client groups are so intense that legislators scarcely have time to weigh their failures. The system is nakedly selfish, but one scarcely expects altruism when slicing the public cake. The occasional altruist who flies dovelike into the congressional shooting galleries does not long survive. The survival, and even growth, of suffering despite the proliferation of public aids is usually the result of redistribution. An increase in Social Security, for example, is accompanied by a rise in the payroll tax paid by young people and their employers. The young people, who are thus less able to survive, need mortgage subsidies. The employer, confronted with higher labor costs from his added payroll tax, therefore employs fewer people. The resulting joblessness thus necessitates public relief, and so on. Each program makes waves. The ramifications pile up on other programs and other groups, all of whom are struggling to stay afloat. All these ramifications are inadequately considered, and the spiritual impact of subsidies and aids is totally ignored. The entire structure has been erected purely on economic and materialistic considerations, and woe to the man whose heart is anguished by any of it. The vaunted humane politics is scarcely humane—not when it ignores the spiritual, religious, emotional, and social hungers of the run of men.

It has been widely remarked that governments whose energies are absorbed in countless benevolent programs lose their ability to perform the basic services for which governments are constituted: keeping the peace, securing speedy, fair justice, and implementing defense against foreign aggression. One of the curiosities of the liberal humane politics is that it has paid scant attention to suffering caused by crime and disorder. Indeed, it is even argued that the victims are only getting what they deserve and that the criminals are only doing what is justified under their social circumstance. Who on the left expressed concern for ghetto shopkeepers whose stores were pillaged by rioters? Apparently *their* suffering does not count. The hallmark of the politics of suffering is its selectivity. The sonorous humane cadences are always reserved for the clients of the left, never for suffering outside of the liberal milieu. Nevertheless, a speedy and certain justice is one of the few things governments can do to relieve suffering everywhere. The maintenance of good order is the prerequisite for any humane reform.

The most significant thing about the politics of suffering is that it exists. It took a lengthy process of politicization to steer people away from their traditional ways of handling suffering and to vest their hope in government. Liberalism has assiduously cultivated that political sense in group after group, beginning with labor and working down to the blacks and ethnics and intellectuals and now to the very young and old. The triumph of this politics of hope came at the expense of hope in God and hope in one's own good character. In the heyday of individualism it was scarcely conceivable that any suffering human could find relief for himself in the bosom of the state. Those few who did—who became customs clerks and postal minions—were more often the objects of contempt than admiration. Even as this hope in a pioneer individualism replaced the promises of Christianity, so did the hope in a political process replace the faith people had in their own strength and good character. Both Christian faith and individualism persist in American society, but no longer at the center, and are no longer regarded with esteem.

It is undoubtedly true that politics is the least effective method to escape misery. For the most part the state imposes misery on some to relieve it in others, and that habit usually comes full circle upon all the interest groups. There are also vast domains of grief about which the state can do little unless it resorts to totalist means. Nevertheless, the politics of hope remains the great vogue of our times. The politicians are honored as saints and benefactors. Learned tomes are written by the hundred on the proper juggling of the engines of state. The whole liberal establishment continues its unremitting effort to politicize more groups, to encourage militance on every hand, and to dissuade the poor from relying on the faith of their fathers or the growth of their own good character and genius.

Elsewhere in the nation a disillusionment has set in about the politics of hope. The promises of the politicians have been too hollow too long. College students have discovered the astonishing truth that their future happiness lies in mastering a vocation rather than hassling the police, and so they are cracking their books. The campuses are quiet and busy. All this is seen in liberal quarters as a calamitous development, a return to normalcy. The great engines of liberalism, such as John Gardner's Common Cause, are wrestling with the new "apathy" and trying to politicize the groups once again. From their standpoint, this revulsion against politics, this skepticism of what any legislature or governor can achieve, is a menacing apathy, or worse, an indication of discouragement and repression. Liberals are political animals. In the new apathy they see their own doom.

At this writing, there has been a spate of articles lamenting the deflation of politics and the inward turn of so many Americans. The sudden chill toward all the machinations of politicians and governments is regarded as catastrophic or as some dark Nixonian plot to repress the population. The suggestion is made that frustration is the real cause, that people feel helpless. It is even suggested that we are sliding into another dismal Eisenhower era in which the pursuit of happiness is superseding indulgence in political embroilment.

For my part, I think this return to normalcy is a cause for rejoicing. Politics is such a poor and uncertain cure for our suffering that I have often marveled at its grip on the souls of so many, especially on the young left. Of *course* people are frustrated by politics! What do liberals expect, after they have assiduously politicized competing groups, ultimately creating a massive stalemate? Politics is the god that failed. The Congress is not the comforter and healer of mankind. In the apotheosis of politics, liberals and their political minions have become the principal idolaters of our era, worshiping the strife of faction rather than a most faithful and merciful Lord. We can only hope that, as suffering individuals discover the futility of state help, they will turn to their own inner development and to a renewed faith in their messiah and that the demon of politics can be forever exorcized from their hearts. When that happens there can be a restoration of calm. Good order is the milieu in which to wrench free of our private sufferings and to work out our destinies. Good order is the one thing the state can achieve toward relief of universal suffering. If there is a danger in these times, it is not in the new apathy toward politics and government, but in the prospect that the politically obsessed will find ways of exacerbating the class war and restoring the hatred, envy, discontent, and anger that must characterize a militant politics.

V

The number of Federal programs aimed at alleviating human suffering is simply breathtaking. They form layer upon layer, lapping over each other in some violent, chaotic effort to leave no unhappiness in any human heart anywhere—and no voter ungrateful. There are benefactions for everyone, even though not everyone makes use of what is available to him.

For the aged there are welfare, Social Security, Medicare, special tax breaks, veterans' pensions, funeral allowances, geriatric research, food stamps, recreation programs, and surplus commodities. For the poor there are welfare, county relief, aid to dependent mothers, Headstart, community action programs, Vista, immunization programs, manpower training, night school, vocational schools, adult literacy programs, regional mental health services, food stamps, equal opportunity laws, aids to the blind and mute, minimum wage laws, tax breaks, subsidized housing, mortgage aids, job placement services, and old folks' homes, ad infinitum. For students there are low-interest loans, scholarships, the GI bill, and drug abuse programs, not to mention free or reduced tuition. For veterans, there are old soldiers' homes, pensions, VA hospitals, job placement services, widows' benefits, and other allowances. In addition to all these there are orphanages, day-care centers, tax abatements, homes for delinquents, work-study programs, agricultural subsidies, tariff protections, export subsidies, government protection of labor monopolies, medical research, benefits for the arts and sciences, and black capitalism programs. The catalogue is as thick as a metropolitan telephone directory.

Many of the programs do alleviate suffering. Older people need their pensions. Fatherless families need support. The unskilled benefit from job training. Medical research benefits the diseased. The contention is not that these programs do no good, but that they are inefficient and frequently do harm, as well. They often usurp superior private options, especially in the realm of insurance and pensions. Such programs must be weighed against the hypothetical prospect of a greatly reduced tax load for all and the proven abilities of private enterprise to cope with needs. An ideology that makes the state the sole vehicle of relief of suffering is an ideology that is blind and heartless, no matter how it trumpets its humanitarianism.

The argument is sometimes advanced that, if suffering persists despite these programs, then what is needed is much more government. Never has that contention seemed so questionable, if not absurd. The net effect of a massive increase in all these programs would be the pauperization of the nation rather than the elimination of suffering. The ultimate result would be a government that does everything, usually by force. It would invade those remaining areas now considered sacrosanct in a free society. We still assume our liberty to govern our lives as we see fit and to suffer the consequences of our follies and reap the rewards of our wisdom. It is certainly possible for governments to invade these areas and offer us relief from our foolishness. The price, however, is beyond comprehension, especially in the realm of such intangibles as our self-esteem, our maturity, our unselfishness, and our courage. What must result is a generation of children, stunted by our protection, cloistered because the state has taken the veil.

There are some on the left who see the prospect of the total state clearly, but nevertheless accept it as the only way to assure the comforts and securities they prefer. Their apostle is behaviorist B. F. Skinner, who has blueprinted a world without liberty and has not shrunk from the consequences of his totalist objective. It is his mystical vision that men must be controlled by controllers and that they will suffer until they surrender their freedom, which is a mythical and ego-supporting concept. Skinner's views have great currency among the zealots of the New Left and within the academy. It is the logical outgrowth and extension of a liberalism that has put its blind faith in the power of the state.

For the rest of us who still treasure our freedom and our right to mature amidst trouble, there arises a need for some criteria to gauge the effectiveness of government. Because suffering is so difficult to measure, it cannot simply be argued that governments should cease their relief when their efforts produce more pain than help. There are no mathematical equations for distress, no way to approach the problem from the standpoint of the social sciences. It is a matter for humane philosophers. Perhaps the best foundation available to us is the assumption of the founding fathers that governments are established to create order and justice, and all the rest is parsley.

Some types of suffering can be relieved naturally by the state. Governments can, for example, interpose between a lynch mob and a suffering black man, prosecute criminals with vigor, and maintain a strong system of defense. There are, however, other types of suffering governments can alleviate only by distorting their basic function. They can, for example, hire poverty provocateurs to arouse the militance of the poor and organize that militance into pressure groups to lever Congress. They can dispatch a Peace Corpsman to far off Boolaboola to teach suffering villagers the rudiments of sanitation. Beyond this, there are areas of suffering that the state can scarcely touch unless it resorts to grotesque acrobatics. What can the state do to help the suffering of those who have lost a loved one or of those who are deeply depressed by their failure in life?

Of course, a state *could* do something about a widow's grief. It could dispatch professional sympathizers. It could provide a doctor armed with sedatives. It could speed a large check to the widow as compensation for her grief. It could parade a collection of new husband prospects before her eyes from its Computerized Matrimony Service. All that is grotesque, an abomination that offends our sensibilities. More important, it denies the widow her legitimate need to grieve, to feel loss, to express her devotion to her beloved. It denies her, more precisely, her right to suffer, a right that should be an inalienable part of our free heritage. Thus, there are realms that the prudent state must not enter. We can discern these, not through any mechanical axioms, but only instinctively as our basic decency dictates. The sense of what is allowable will vary from person to person, but it will surely unify around the general need to kick out the government when the bureaucrats become apostles of hell.

So strange are the times that it is not always easy to find a consensus favoring vigorous government in the realm of justice and order. Fashionable people have no particular concern about the victims of crime or disorder, not even when the victims themselves are black. A shrug of the shoulders dismisses the sufferings of innumerable victims of crime and mayhem whose lives and property are threatened by the government's failure to maintain good order. The same casual shrug is reserved for the suffering that results from their own pet programs: Social Security, for example. It can be a mixed blessing for those who receive it.

It can mean austere independence, but it can also demolish the happy three-generation family and impose an awesome loneliness on the aged. The very old have a special rapport with the very young. In a three-generation family the old have the happy task of babysitting the young, educating the children, and spoiling them in a dozen happy ways. They are useful to their children and they share love at the daily breaking of bread. They are not cast aside, forgotten, alone, waiting for a merciful death; rather, they are an integral part of family life, with contributions to make. But this is the sort of thing rarely considered by the fashionable liberals with their brittle humanitarianism. If they were capable of weighing all programs in the light of the liabilities as well as the assets they carry, they would not be so certain of their moral superiority.

Most people, including those on the left, can readily conceptualize a totalitarian government, but not many leftists understand the idea that government can be merely grotesque. A perverse state is one that tries to be merciful and succeeds in being merciless, a state that tries to heal suffering only to spread misery. I am not talking about tyranny here, but simply the perversity of spreading misery while attempting good. Increasingly, the Federal government is grotesque rather than oppressive. The perverse state pierces those areas we regard as sacred and personal. It interferes with our joy in sharing the problems of others. Our mature joy in carrying each other's burdens is an area of private life we have always sequestered from the state. It has no business there, but it is just at this frontier that our happiness is threatened most. This is the point where public servants may not tread and politicians may not enter, the point where the state becomes an abomination. I think of my right to err, to fail, to grow, to love, to reach others, to give and receive, to submit my sufferings to my God, to endure cold, poverty, pain and hunger if I choose, and to wrestle with my devils without the assistance of political messiahs. Our right to suffer needs defending—not that we enjoy suffering, but because it is a part of a larger process that makes mature men and women of us.

A public that understands its sufferings and their value is best equipped to impose limits on the liberal state and its political acolytes. In its eagerness to accept the newest subsidies, the public too often overlooks the intangibles that add up to misery or joy. An entire generation has now imbibed with its mother's milk a belief in political solutions. It is a generation that can define its sorrows readily enough, but it then takes the critical, unthinking leap into politics for the answers. There needs to be light focused on that leap. That bridge, that ganglion that connects private grief with public solutions deserves attention. A man suffers; he is black, or old, or infirm, or poor. His suffering shoots impulses through that ganglion, that gateway into politics, and he lays his burdens on the doorstep of Congress, where they inevitably compete with the burdens of others. No one has told him that there are other gateways to other solutions. It is always politics, and never God, or the evolution of his character, or the application of free capitalism. Obviously, there is feedback from the political arena through the ganglion into the man's heart. He may be helped to some degree, but not too much. The prevalent restlessness is testimony to the impotence of government. Moreover, the feedback from the world of politics is not always welcome.

Once a subsidy or service is obtained, it must be defended against other predators and against inflation. The individual's relief is also his pain; he must agitate to keep it and expand it. And so the battle rages, class against class, group against group. That is the politics of suffering. The only certain thing about it is that the state will not abolish individual misery and that it will only create universal misery if it attempts the impossible.

VI

Christians believe that some, but not all, suffering is the result of sin: that is, that suffering is the result of moral disorders within people, as well as of other calamities. Christians purge sin by confessing it, by repenting their errors and lusts, and by affirming their faith in the forgiving Lord. If they fail, they become the slaves of sin, idolators prostrate at the altars of lust, drugs, lucre, hatred, and intolerance. If they seek relief through the state rather than through God, they are not healed.

Sin is an offense against God. To secular men, this concept is at best a myth, at worst a fetter on their individuality. However, they need not light lanterns and peer into murky corners to discover the presence of evil. They will find it in the mansions of the rich as well as the shanties of the poor. They will find the least of it where mature Christians live. Like others, Christians sin and suffer, but they have the means to transcend the cycle of evil, to burst free from the curse of Adam. Christians do suffer, sometimes grievously, but with a curious wild joy, a foolishness of faith and a mad serenity in the midst of defeat. That they carry their cross there can be no doubt, but it is equally certain that their yoke is easy.

A Christian can scarcely call himself by that name unless he believes in the immediacy of God's power. He cannot simply believe that God existed and waned in the shadowy past or that His power is reserved for the misty future. Unless a Christian feels the proximity of God's strength at all times, there is little point to his faith. When he lays his burdens and sufferings before his Lord, it is with the certitude that he will be helped. That aid does not always come the way he hopes and expects; God uses the present to prepare for the future. Sometimes we fail to understand why we suffer, only to discover at a later date that the suffering fitted into an astonishing mosaic of new strength and life. At other times the suffering is lifted directly, as fast as the prayer is offered. Periodically, we are given new courage and faith, but not surcease from our pain, and so we accept our lot with thanksgiving and hope and confidence in a joyous future. Sometimes we see that great healings and wonders follow in the wake of faith as surely as they did in biblical times. We gather our hope and our patience together and find our weakness turned into strength and our foolishness transformed into wisdom.

In the midst of all this we abandon our hope in government and eschew the politics of suffering, with all its clash of wills and ritual greed. There are better ways. We abandon discord and heated polemics and the New Politics with its institutional hatreds of Middle America, business, the establishment, and many other fruitful things. We cannot abandon the state altogether; it has intruded too deeply at some points. We can nevertheless organize our daily lives so as to ignore the state, to work and play and worship and proffer our alms without reference to our governors and their schemes. We can withdraw from all politics and starve the politicians. We can refuse to attend their rallies or endorse their programs, even those we prefer. We can drop out of politics and then organize our lives fruitfully, charitably, and faithfully around the church and the community of the Holy Spirit.

I have given scant attention to individualism as a means of relieving our suffering because that is the precinct of aristocrats. Further, it is not much more effective than politics. It assumes that each of us must overcome his sorrows through main strength and that, as we discipline our minds and bodies and wills, we shall conquer our frustrations. It holds that, by evolving a high moral character, we will do others no ill. This is all true enough; the pursuit of individualism is surely more noble than politics. Strength is admirable; it is the resource of the world's most fortunate. Like Christianity, individualism can use suffering to steel the character and teach endurance. Individualists are dependent neither on the state nor on their special interest groups. They move singly, often countervailing mobs and gangs.

This Nietzchean approach to suffering, however, is for the few who are able to germinate the flowers of their soul alone. Most of us are weaker. Even though we have inherited a lusty pioneer individualism from our forefathers, we have become too civilized, and the world has changed, so that a rampant individuality often produces more suffering among our close-packed masses than conformity. I sense the dilution of my own individuality in these times, and I suspect that a free-spirited individuality will be less and less able to overcome suffering in the future. New casts of mind, drawing on endurance and faith, will be needed to cope with the world of corporations and computers. I admire boundlessly the individualism that built this nation. The toughness was real: it cannot be successfully debunked by cloistered scholars who never faced a hostile wilderness. Since, unlike my ancestors, I cannot marshal my vagrant emotions and intellect into a steely will capable of conquering continents, my hope is in that mighty fortress I call God.

Most of us are too weak to be tough, too weak even to be virtuous most of the time. If we demand more from the state, the state becomes grotesque. If we resist God, we lose hope. If we turn toward the old individualism, we become new sources of friction and bang our heads against an impersonal world. If we try Stoicism, we know no joy. If we resort to Epicureanism, we never discover the spirit of God. If we try to endure, we are ground down. If we permit suffering to pile up, we go mad. We find release only in the green pastures and still waters of faith, where His rod and staff may still comfort us.

2
Lower Than The Angels

I

There is no doctrine of physical equality in Christianity, but that has not deterred liberal philosophers from attempting to derive one. There is a wealth of scriptural material about the rich, the poor, status and power, and the first and the last, but none of it can be readily molded to fit a notion of social justice based on equalization of income and opportunity. This has greatly disappointed the ideologues, and they have come to regard the church's failure to support egalitarian measures as yet another example of the moral inadequacy of a tribal religion that somehow survived the ancient world. After all, the Rousseauian perception of absolute equality in this life is a matter of simple justice, an obvious moral good, a clear beatific vision of a society in which all are kings and none is subordinate to another. Hence, the lack of such a doctrine in Christianity must reveal its imperfect and pre-modern character, or at least its corruption by generations of ruling class clerics and princes. As with the problems of peace, militarism, capitalism, private property, and women's equality, the church's viewpoint on equality of income is "morally inferior."

Nonetheless, because of the richness of the biblical teaching on the subject, there has been a sustained effort to create a social gospel, a Christian socialism that justifies statist leveling with Christian moral teaching. There are, after all, rebukes of the rich in the scriptures and a great deal of teaching about the poor and their needs, about surrendering worldly things, about doing good and loving one's neighbors—all of which, while not exactly egalitarian, would seem, at least, to support a program of redistribution of incomes, or "soaking the rich." Indeed, is this not the core of faith? And if there is no specific egalitarian concept in Christianity, is it not true that one is implied, that God will protect and comfort the poor, who are morally superior to the greedy rich? Indeed, how can there be a joyous, serene world if there are needy people anywhere, especially when they are mixed with the affluent? Is not such inequality

34

the source of the scourge of war? Thus, the notion persists: Christianity whole-heartedly supports all efforts to create equality, and the more pristine that equality seems to be, the more it includes income, opportunity, and status, the more Christian it is. The purest Christianity of all would see to it that income is divided to the last cent and that no one rises an iota above his neighbor. In fact, however, while most democrats of the left insist that such equality is the ultimate ideal, they would be content with minor variations for the sake of some diversity and a degree of freedom. Equality nevertheless remains the ideal, even if practicality sometimes intervenes to compel the bestowal of honors and incentives on men of talent.

So there has arisen a large modern school of Christian egalitarians who range from outright socialists to routine democratic liberals seeking a welfare state that guarantees income for all. While these doctrinaires do not reject charity, they are restless with it and consider it impractical in a mass industrial society. Their real interest is statist welfare, which can confiscate the booty of the rich, who acquired their wealth by nefarious means, and restore the ill-gotten gains to the poor and oppressed through welfare, education, job-training, pensions, and grants, all in the name of Jesus Christ.

Unfortunately, the business of ramming the Christian faith into a socialistic straitjacket is infinitely more difficult than it first appears. It is easy enough to pirate a few verses of scripture to support the whole socialist enterprise, but brutally hard to squeeze an egalitarian doctrine out of a religion that expressly rejects coercive efforts to establish material equality on earth among men. The problems of the socialists are deepened by an expressly antiegalitarian cast to much of scripture, including the teachings of the Lord, the elaborations of the apostles, and the positing of a true Christian scheme of justice based on God's love for all. That is to say, the larger portion of Christian teachings deals with an unequal world, where there are unequal talents, unequal character, unequal wealth, and unequal learning, all of which are regarded as the natural condition of mankind, arising from biological, cultural, environmental, and adventitious circumstances. The real thrust of the faith is not toward eliminating such inequities, but toward widening love and fraternity within the world as it is, thus mitigating the differing conditions of man without destroying variety. To leap from concepts of love embedded at the root of Christianity to concepts of equality or calculated social justice is to take a fateful step away from religion toward secular egalitarianism—indeed, toward a doctrine built directly on envy, for that is the nature of egalitarianism. If no man coveted his neighbor's goods or his wife or his wealth, then social justice would be devoid of meaning. Most of the thrust toward equality today is rooted in covetousness; actual concern for the poor has little to do with it and nothing at all to do with fleecing the rich.

There is such a profusion of biblical teaching and doctrine about poverty and wealth and status that it cannot be covered comprehensively here. It is still necessary to build a substantial case, in part because the historic thrust of Christianity has been greatly distorted in recent times, creating skepticism about what the church has really taught for most of the centuries of its life. For example, the church does not teach a simple doctrine of hostility to wealth. Its teachings are

35

far more complex and have much to do with what wealth does to the souls of those who possess it. At no point in all Christian teaching is there justification for confiscating wealth; indeed, this would be regarded as theft. The souls of the wealthy are not improved by being deprived of their goods, but by a voluntary and loving surrender of some of their surplus to those who need it. Moreover, the confiscation of wealth would be motivated by covetousness, which is a sin directly proscribed by the tenth commandment. Of course, the wealthy have special and heavy responsibilities, which will be discussed at length later, but what they do through fraternal love is not comparable with what follows when their riches are taken from them. Robin Hood was not a Christian.

An incident described in the gospel of Matthew is instructive. A wealthy young man asks Jesus what he must do to gain eternal life. Jesus tells him to keep the commandments, and the young man replies that he has done so all his life. Jesus then tells him that, if he would be perfect, he must sell his possessions and give them to the poor, "and you will have treasure in heaven; and come, follow me." The youth leaves sorrowfully because he is rich, and it is difficult to surrender what he has. Jesus then explains to his disciples that it is hard for a rich man to enter into heaven; indeed, harder than for a camel (or a rope) to pass through the eye of a needle. When his disciples object to the harshness of such a situation, Jesus replies that God can save even the rich. (19:16-26)

The incident is important because it establishes wealth as an impediment to the salvation of the wealthy, a danger to the souls of those who put their trust in money and accumulations. There is nothing in the teaching that suggests that wealth is inherently evil, only that it causes spiritual difficulties, and nothing that validates confiscating that wealth on behalf of the poor. Jesus did not order the youth to dispose of his wealth. Such a confiscation misses the point, which has to do with the owner's attitude toward his riches. If his wealth is simply confiscated, it does not change the owner's allegiance to mammon or dispose him toward God. On the contrary, it embitters him. The point is religious and spiritual, rather than social: it does not contemplate redistribution or weigh the question of equality. It has to do only with a man's relationship to God.

This Christian viewpoint is reinforced by St. James, who has scathing words for the greedy rich:

Come now, you rich, weep and howl for the miseries that are coming upon you. Your riches have rotted and your garments are motheaten. Your gold and silver have rusted, and their rust will be evidence against you and will eat your flesh like fire. You have laid up treasure for the last days. Behold the wages of the laborers who mowed your fields, which you kept back by fraud, cry out; and the cries of the harvesters have reached the ears of the Lord of hosts. You have lived on the earth in luxury and in pleasure; you have fattened your hearts in a day of slaughter. You have condemned, you have killed the righteous man; he does not resist you.

This warning to the unjust rich is framed in terms of the soul, the jeopardized life with God. Gold and silver do not physically rust, but metaphorically riches do not last as long as the soul. So the rich are warned that their fraud and avarice will be dealt with by God. It is a severe warning, but it is not couched in terms of equality or confiscating wealth; neither does it suggest that affluence itself is evil or that poverty is somehow virtuous. It is not posed as a problem for the state. Indeed, the whole thrust of New Testament teaching excludes the state because it is not really relevant to Christian virtue and faith.

The plainspoken, charitable James was particularly aware of the poor and God's special concern about their souls. James asks: "Has not God chosen those who are poor in the world to be rich in faith and heirs to the kingdom which he has promised to those who love him?" Here again James is talking about the condition of the soul, and he describes God's compensation to the poor as richness of faith that will enable them to enter the kingdom of heaven. This is a very different idea from one that promises the poor economic equality or any sort of physical riches. What we begin to discover in James is an aversion toward the love of wealth, a love rooted in avarice, greed, hunger for prestige or success, all of which can separate a man from God. Indeed, James warns against giving special status or honor to the wealthy, for example, by providing a well-dressed man with favored seats while compelling a shabby one to sit in an inferior spot.

In one of his parables, Jesus describes a rich man whose land yields well, so he decides to build a bigger barn to store his crops and then live easily on his wealth. But God says to him, "Fool! This night your soul is required of you; and the things you have prepared, whose will they be?" The man's covetousness kept him from being rich toward God. Again, the problem is not wealth *per se,* but the storing of it. Hoarded wealth offends God, Who wants to see the riches back in service and to see men trust his providence. In the following verses Jesus warned against anxiety: "For life is more than food and the body more than clothing." (Luke 12:22) "Fear not, little flock. . . . Sell your possessions, give alms; provide yourselves with purses that do not grow old, with a treasure in the heavens that does not fail, where no thief approaches and no moth destroys. For where your treasure is, there will your heart be also." Again there appears the obvious concern with the soul. By clinging to transient wealth, which is a false and destructible idol, the soul misses the true and permanent love of God.

The theme of the threat of wealth to the soul is continued elsewhere in Luke: "No servant can serve two masters; for either he will hate the one and love the other, or he will be devoted to the one and despise the other. You cannot serve God and Mammon." Here again, this teaching of Jesus is not at all concerned with social inequities, but rather with an individual's slavery to wealth and moneygrubbing. The question whether society should permit the rich to exist does not interest Him. The question whether the wealth should be forcibly distributed to those at the bottom of the income scale does not enter into his religion. His approach to wealth, as with all his teachings, is intensely personal. The love of wealth can corrode a man and alienate him from higher values and from God, and that is infinitely more important than any social abstraction about equality or economic justice.

Indeed, the social egalitarians have a serious problem demonstrating that their doctrines have anything to do with the insight of Jesus. They are forced to derive an egalitarian ethic, not from anything Jesus may have said about equality, but from His warnings that the rich imperil their souls. Egalitarianism is not implied in Christian doctrine. There are serious obstacles to it, especially the commandment prohibiting covetousness and all the warnings against envy. Both of these dark forces in the soul lie at the root of efforts to reduce all of mankind to a single plain, although they often masquerade as compassion. The commandment recorded in Exodus is one of the most frequently ignored and violated of the ten: "You shall not covet your neighbor's house; you shall not covet your neighbor's wife, or his manservant, or his maidservant, or his ox, or his ass, or anything that is your neighbor's." In short, you shall not establish your own sense of worth by comparing yourself and your possessions to those of others. The commandment presupposes material inequalities: there would be no sense to it if all men had the same possessions. It is, precisely, a commandment to dampen the dark lusts of those who have not and who wish to take what others have. To be sure, men with exactly equal possessions could still covet others' goods and wives, but the real thrust of the commandment is against the egalitarian spirit. It is a commandment with vast implications and innumerable pitfalls, and it is a worthy guide through the modern materialist world. It goes hand in hand with the commandment against stealing as props for a natural—that is, unequal—social order.

II

There is more to poverty than a lack of income or possessions. It is a Christian insight that the poor include all who are deprived in one way or another, including those who have emotional, physical, material and spiritual needs. The desperation of the poor extends far beyond money: indeed, some of the poorest souls on earth are those who lack love. Some never married or have lost a spouse. Some have spouses, but their relationship has died so that each starves alone. Others have lost children or parents or they never had the chance for family life and parental love. Some men were abandoned by their wives. Others may be prisoners. The blind and deaf are among the poor, as well as the disfigured and limbless and the plain. Some of the most impoverished are mad or at least disturbed—people who drive others away, who cannot trust anyone, who reject God and charity or never admit to imperfection, failure, folly, or any lacks.

The ignorant are poor: misled, beguiled, foolish, and vulnerable to exploiters. The orphaned are poor, deprived of the parental love and home life that build security and happiness. The diseased are poor, unable to function, to live, to escape pain. Some are poor because of external circumstances: depression, layoffs, a trade overrun by technology, a livelihood that no longer yields a living. The elderly are sometimes poor, burdened with failing bodies and an isolated life with a dwindling future. Poor are the chronically slothful or those who cannot drive themselves to produce according to their aspirations. Some of the retired are poor because they have little to do. So the poor include an almost endless variety of those who suffer; in Christian terminology they are grouped as the *poor in spirit*. God is especially concerned about all of these, and not merely those who suffer from low incomes alone, although low income often goes hand in hand with other spiritual and physical poverty.

If, as Christian teaching indicates, true poverty is a matter of being deprived, then it is obvious that mere economic redistribution—the leftist formula—is quite inadequate and scarcely begins to alleviate the problem. For the poor, above all, are victims of a state of mind that results from being crushed by life. The truly poor are those who have given up, whose will is faltering, whose inner resources have finally succumbed to the avalanche of fate. There comes a point in life when it is impossible to carry on or struggle further, not because the will dies a cowardly death, but because it is overwhelmed by bitter life. It is not something a strong will or good character or great perseverance can overcome. The most rugged individualists are regularly overcome by personal catastrophes that sweep them under with the force of tidal waves. The notion that the strong individualist can always triumph over brutal destiny is a myth, although courage surely helps and an inner resilience works miracles. In all our cities, as well as in the countryside, there are aging as well as young persons who have given up, who live in cubicles as vegetables, waiting for the mercy of death. They are the demolished men to whom God promises hope.

When John the Baptist sent disciples inquiring whether Jesus was the messiah, his response was in some ways peculiar. "Go and tell John what you hear and see," Jesus replied. "The blind receive their sight and the lame walk, lepers are cleansed and the deaf hear, and the dead are raised up and the poor have good news preached to them. And blessed is he who takes no offense at me." (Mat. 11:4) That answer always offends leftist clerics, as well as secular liberals, because it makes it clear that Jesus was merely preaching "good news" to the poor instead of organizing charities or advocating redistribution of income. Preaching to the poor was indeed a strange thing to do when, in fact, the poor needed sustenance. It is true that he had healed all sorts of maladies and restored physical senses, thus helping those impoverished in these ways, but as for the poor—he preached to them! He *preached!* And this is about as annoying a notion as any materialist liberal can tolerate. Were not the poor perhaps the last group that needed to be preached to, morally superior to the rich? Were they not common men, free of all the chicanery and vice of the powerful and privileged classes? Why not preach to the rich? Why not rebuke the powerful?

It was clear that Jesus had something infinitely greater in mind than mere economic organization on behalf of the poor. What he understood was their desperation, their feeling of being something less than human. He knew that many had surrendered the will to live and flourish. They had lost hope, and with the demise of hope they had entered into living death, subsisting until their hearts stopped beating, mercifully sooner than the hearts of other men. So the good news, or the Gospel, that Jesus preached was that of God's love and concern. It was necessary to revive hope before any real healing could occur. It was necessary to convey God's rich promises to awaken a desire to live, to struggle, to acquire self-esteem. That is to say, Jesus treated the poor as human beings rather than as economic objects in liberal blueprints. He preached that God cares and that there is hope and healing for all the poor in spirit who have faith in a caring God. Indeed, he preached that "Blessed are the poor in spirit, for theirs is the kingdom of heaven." And so it was that Jesus put first things first, reaching into the souls of the poor to revive life and hope with God's promises for both this life and the next. Blessed are the poor in spirit. It is a breathtaking approach to poverty compared to that of the socialists, one that takes desperate individual humans and cups them in love and hope and wipes away their tears and comforts them and restores the will to live. It is a relationship, moreover, strictly between a poor man and God, that can flourish without the aid of any other mortal, although the charity of others is vitally important in restoring life to the poor. Jesus had an understanding of poverty that shames the miserable, barren socialist redistribution of income, the venomous egalitarianism that is the alpha and omega of leftist liberals.

Jesus never advocated socialism. He never proposed governmental redistribution of income or penalizing the rich. He never suggested that his goal was physical equality, or communism, or public ownership of production. In fact, everything in scripture suggests that these were all anathema to him and irrelevant. He did teach a doctrine of love and compassion that would ensure the care of the needy, as well as the incorporation of the isolated poor into the Christian community. He elaborated the idea of fraternal concern. He charged the rich with special obligations in their treatment of those less fortunate. However, there is not a word, not a phrase, not a verse among his teachings to support physical equality. The position of Christian liberals is based on desperate derivations of an alleged ethic that exists nowhere.

The Christian approach to poverty is comprehensive, rather than materialistic. Jesus approached the problem from a direction entirely at odds with the dogmas of socialism: He began with the Gospel, the "good news," the support and love of God for the defeated. He planted faith and hope first. The recovery from impoverishment of any sort would begin in that good soil. Once the spirit is restored, faith rebuilt, and the burdens of sin removed, the healing of the body is necessary, and after that the improvement of physical circumstances and the restoration of loving relationships to others. The general restorative plan used by Jesus involved the spirit first, then the body, then the community of others, and finally improvement in physical surroundings and conditions. Liberalism and socialism approach poverty from the reverse side, beginning— and usually ending—with a welfare dole or egalitarian measures, plus some job training or education for those who are educable. This ignores the spirit. It is better than nothing and does some good, but any healing is adventitious, mere happenstance, because the broken spirit of the poor is never touched. The approach is symbolized by the great housing projects that now lie abandoned or demolished because the poor who were moved into them remained poor in spirit even amid pleasant physical surroundings. It is evident that many crushed spirits do not respond to welfare, job training, or even health care. Such brutalized spirits, so common among the wounded blacks, remain crumpled and broken even when material comforts and opportunities are proffered by the state. But Jesus' approach, which reaches directly to the broken spirit of the poor with the promise of God's love, with hope, with freedom from sin, with life, health, and reunion with God, coaxes the broken heart back to life.

The spirit is at the center of man. It must be healed first before material aid can have a lasting impact. This is not to suggest that the secular approach is a total failure or entirely wrong. The body must be sustained in any case, and basic amenities build a necessary base for a better life. But the overall failure is evident in mounting welfare rolls and the incapacity of the system to move people out of dependency. The failure is also evident in the spread of despair and alienation, in the weak character of so many of the young, in so many welfare families in which dependence is bequeathed from generation to generation, and in the spread of crime and disorder. The materialistic approach rarely heals; it only sustains life at its lowest ebb.

That Jesus had in mind for the poor something radically larger than liberalistic welfare is evident in his description of those who will inherit the kingdom of heaven. "Come, O blessed of my Father, inherit the kingdom that was prepared for you from the foundations of the world; for I was hungry and you gave me food, I was thirsty and you gave me drink, I was a stranger and you welcomed me, I was naked and you clothed me, I was sick and you visited me, I was in prison and you came to me." Half of these examples of charity extend beyond material need into the realm of love and sociability.

There is a famous passage in the epistle of James, however, that makes it clear that preaching is not enough; there must also be real, physical, material charity, a transfer of goods to those in need. "What does it profit, my brethren, if a man says he has faith but has not works? Can his faith save him? If a brother or sister is ill-clad and in lack of daily food, and one of you says to them, 'Go in peace, be warmed and filled,' without giving them the things needed for the body, what does it profit?" (2:14) Note that the thrust of the passage is religious; it insists that, to be saved, a Christian must add works to faith. Thus again, the concern of the passage is with the condition of the soul, of the relationship of the soul to God, which is at the heart of Christian religion. To be charitable is to put the soul into a good relationship with God. This is not a scheme of secular welfare, nor a scheme of saintly altruism, because it posits a very personal motive— salvation—for charity. James reinforces the religious nature of his argument by asserting that pure and undefiled religion amounts to visiting orphans and widows in their affliction and keeping one's self unstained from the world. (1:27)

These ordinances of Christianity are in the nature of personal mandates, which is the standard approach throughout the New Testament. There is nothing social or governmental about them. If a social gospel is to be derived from such personal mandates, it can be done only inferentially and derivatively by assuming that the Christian instructions for salvation of the soul are applicable to societies and can be channeled through governments.

There is a real problem in extending such instructions for personal salvation into a dialectic that supports statist welfare. Since governments have no souls and cannot be saved, the essence of the teachings about charity shift from the realm of personal behavior to institutional obligations. On the other hand, the charities organized by the corporate church are another matter, because the church is a body of those souls seeking salvation, and such voluntary charities are simply the organization of many such individual impulses arising spontaneously from the love and mercy of individuals. There is no shift in the essence. St. James can scarcely urge a government to supply food to the hungry on the ground that the government's soul would thereby benefit, but he can indeed urge church members to be charitable. So the ethic perforce undergoes mutation on its way to socialism, and what emerges is not voluntary giving, sustained by love and mercy, but rather welfare sustained by taxes, that is to say, by moneys wrested coercively from people and disbursed by paid bureaucrats, whose motive is hardly love, on the basis of legal claims and eligibility rather than fundamental need. How often are the most desperate entirely ineligible for statist relief of any sort!

If Jesus or any of his apostles had such a mutation ultimately in mind as the end, the goal, of all Christian teaching, as the utopia on the Christian horizon, they would have said so plainly; it was not their habit to conceal the future or to mince words or to hide the ultimate purpose of the new faith. In fact, no such scheme of government welfare was ever contemplated or desired. Welfare, which is a dole without love, usually alienates and isolates the recipients, drives them out of sight and mind, renders them invisible, and thus desensitizes Christian compassion. It supports the bodies, but ostracizes the personalities, of its recipients. It fosters antagonism and envy and bitterness among those who receive it. They need the dollars, but their souls hunger for love, for notice, for any sort of care. Welfarism leaves its victims suspended in a limbo of isolation, unloved, resented, and even more deprived than they were previously. To suppose that such a scheme was the final goal, the direction of all Christian progress, is gravely to misunderstand Christianity.

Although the church fathers did not consider charity in the context of government activity, they did consider it as a function of the organized church. Thus, St. Paul commended the churches of Macedonia for their organized generosity: "For they gave according to their means, as I can testify, and beyond their means, of their own free will, begging us earnestly for the favor of taking part in the relief of the saints—and this, not as we expected, but first they gave themselves to the Lord and to us by the will of God." (II Cor. 8:3) Paul goes on to urge the Corinthians to make similar sacrifices as a corporate church enterprise. Obviously, organized charity arising from church bodies is essentially the same as private charity by individual Christians. It is voluntary, arising in the free will, springing from goodness and mercy and an eagerness for salvation. No matter how humane governmental welfare may seem, it does not fit any of these categories. It is based more on an avoidance of charity than on an expression thereof. It is grounded on an abstract sense of responsibility rather than on fraternal love. Its principal benefit is not to the recipients, but to the politicians, who speciously appear to be charitable by promoting the distribution of other people's money, extracted through taxes.

Because Christianity is a religion and not a social blueprint, donations play a key role in the approach to God. Thus, writes St. Paul, a giver is rewarded by God; indeed, a giver never misses what he gives. "The point is this: he who has sown sparingly will also reap sparingly, and he who sows bountifully will also reap bountifully. Each one must do as he has made up his mind, not reluctantly or under compulsion, for God loves a cheerful giver. And God is able to provide you with every blessing in abundance, so that you may always have enough of everything and may provide in abundance for every good work." (II Cor.

9:6) There, indeed, is the miracle: we shall not miss what we give, if we give in abundance and cheerfully. So God provides for the poor in a most astonishing way, by restoring the goods of the charitable, by repaying givers. It takes faith to believe that. Unlike welfarism, charity does good to the giver. Charity does as much for the souls and hearts of the givers as it does for the recipients! On the other hand, welfarism only deprives the donors of spiritual and material advancement. It cheats everybody. It is not Christian, nor does it derive from any Christian ethic.

III

For some philosophers and theologians there is a particular voluptuousness in the idea of material equality. They perceive the matter as simple justice: whoever has been deprived of the chance to earn money or accumulate wealth equally with others has simply been cheated by life, or perhaps by the rich, or by the upper classes and rulers. The idea of equality is seductive, although few of its adherents go so far as to insist on absolute equalization of income and possessions. They would be content with a universal middle class—why *is* it that they also hate the bourgeois?—where the chance to rise to affluence is curtailed and subsidies are offered to all who slip below the median.

The result of this obsession with putative social justice is a massive, manifold effort to level mankind, almost entirely through government methods. There are progressive taxes; heavy inheritance duties; varieties of welfare and relief; an infinity of pension and unemployment programs; different kinds of education and cultural enrichment; and special poverty programs. There is remedial learning for the deprived, but rank hostility to private schools or to any education that might give the brilliant child what is regarded as an unfair advantage. Of course, very little of all this works: men have a way of sorting themselves out so that strong and weak character, intelligence and stupidity, education and ignorance all affect incomes. It is difficult, indeed, for the egalitarian to suppress the natural inequalities of men or overcome the aspirations of families to perpetuate themselves by bequeathing wealth through future generations. In fact, the failures of the egalitarians only generate the lust to impose harsher controls, and thus we witness a vicious circle of failure triggering new repression that in turn triggers failure. Loopholes become the salvation of civilized diversity. Indeed, life proceeds through those excoriated loopholes. To impose the equality of the ants and bees upon us, it is only necessary to close a few amiable loopholes. We are only a few loopholes away from the Maoist revolution in any case. One should go to bed at night thanking God for the tax exemptions for the blind, for the privilege of deducting interest on our little castles, for the untaxed churches, for the tax deductions available for people who move, for the local autonomy resulting from tax-free municipal bonds, and for the freedom to send our children to private schools.

What is unbearable to the social Maoists is that people come in such an infinite variety, with endless combinations of intelligence, character, strength, and courage. Worse, they are reared in mansions and shacks, in broods of one to perhaps a dozen, with means ranging from survival to opulence. Furthermore, some parents are intelligent and educated, and their fortunate offspring inherit the benefit. Moreover, some youngsters are victims of happenstance and accidents, all of which upsets the apple cart of equality. Some people even win the Irish Sweepstakes! Even more insidious is the fact that some people are actually happy, while others are constantly miserable. God's natural inequalities seem perverse, mad, cruel, and something to be remedied at once by civilization. It is bad enough for individuals to differ, but perfectly abominable that whole nations differ, not only in material success, but in achievement as well.

To the delight of those who love diverse men instead of monotonous Man, the world can never be cured of its variety. The uniqueness, folly, wisdom, surprisingness of men cannot be erased, even by an appalling totalitarianism. There is a certain sensitive type of liberal "Christian" who professes to be horrified by all the extremes of wealth and misery he sees jumbled up together. He is also dismayed by the New Testament, which has so little to say about inequalities. He expects there to find the fountainhead of social justice, but he finds only strange, old tribal doctrines about coveting neighbors' maidservants and wives. He searches in vain for something—anything—that the Messiah or his apostles said or did that could be transformed into a good modern doctrine of social redistribution. That, after all, is the crux of the matter: what good is Christianity if it fails to meet today's ethical requirements and social needs? How can there be a good society if men are not equal? Somewhere, in all that welter of New Testament thought, there must be a doctrine underpinning the progressive income tax or a moral basis for the Office of Economic Opportunity. After all, what good is faith, or God, when a man is hungry?

Eventually, he will discover in Luke that Christianity does have a doctrine about fairness and equality. But what a doctrine! According to Luke, "One of the multitude said to Him, 'Teacher, bid my brother divide the inheritance with me.' And He said to him, 'Man, who made me a judge or a divider over you?' And He said to them, 'Take heed, and beware of all covetousness; for a man's life does not consist in the abundance of his possessions.'" (Luke 12:13) Consider: Jesus not only refused to share the wealth, dividing it between the have and have-not brothers, but he rebuked the covetousness of the brother who came to him, and probably the other brother also. By rejecting "fairness" and "equality" he must remain the despair of liberals and socialists alike. He followed that pointed rebuke with a parable about a rich man who accumulated wealth only to die before he could spend it, the implication being that wealth is a transitory advantage, less valuable than eternal life.

All that is scarcely what the egalitarian has in mind. He would have been much happier if Jesus had divided the wealth and had then delivered a little homily about making all men financially equal. If Jesus had done that, he could have been the model for the whole egalitarian movement that has been growing since before the French Revolution. Jesus would have been the prototype for the compassionate liberal lawmaker, dividing the wealth between haves and have-nots; the standard for the benevolent United Nations, shipping wealth from the rich countries to the poor; and the model for the glorification of the Common Man, forever taking away the possessions of the one who steps above the mass of men and giving them to simpler souls.

Instead, He chastised the disinherited fellow. Utterly astonishing! He sent him away empty-handed. Amazing! Is it the case, then, that there is no justice inherent in Christianity? Of course not. There is a profound concept of justice and compensation, based not so much on equality as on the rewarding of good endeavor and the punishment of the evil, something we will examine later. What is so difficult for the egalitarians—both secular and "Christian"—to grasp is that a true Christian doctrine has nothing to do with equal incomes. The poor in spirit are greater in number than the indigent, and God's love must embrace them all. He deals, not with an abstraction called the poor, defined as a lower percentage of the society, but with alcoholics, prisoners, widows, orphans, lunatics, those unable to hold jobs, the blind, basket cases, war victims, cancer patients, heroin addicts, foreigners in a strange land, and the loveless. Divine justice has the awesome task of helping each of these to carry his cross, to overcome his trouble, and to compensate for permanent loss. How greatly God must have loved Helen Keller. What is God to do? Throw silver and gold at all these underprivileged? Soon after the death and resurrection, Peter and John were accosted by a lame beggar near the temple gate. Peter said to him, "I have no silver and gold, but I give you what I have: in the name of Jesus Christ of Nazareth, walk." And the man walked, and then began to leap and praise God. A leftist would have given the beggar gold, if anything.

The well-known parable of the talents suggests a Christian justice based on what each of us does with the assets and liabilities given to us or imposed on us. Jesus describes a situation in which a master, about to embark on a journey, gives one employee five talents, another two talents, and another only a single talent, "each according to his ability." The able man earns five more; the less able one earns two more; but the one given only one talent buries it and thus earns nothing with it. The master returns and demands an accounting. He rewards the two who made the best possible use of what they were given, but he casts out angrily the fellow who buried his talent. The parable is a description of the kingdom of heaven and describes one aspect of God's justice. Those who receive great gifts and good fortune in life are expected to use them well. Those whose circumstances are more mixed are also expected to do the best they can, and even those who receive little are expected to do what they can with what they are given. The parable, like all Christian doctrine, never supposes that people are equal. The only sense of equality derives from a judgment based on what each received. God expects less, that is, from those who in life had less opportunity or were heavily beseiged by difficulties and tragedies. "For to everyone who has will more be given," Jesus concludes, "and he will have abundance; but from him who has not, even what he has will be taken away." Now, of course, that is not about the poor. There is nothing in the New Testament to suggest that the poor will, or should have, what little they possess taken away. It is about the use made of God's gifts. If a man who has wealth and love and happiness shares these with the less fortunate, he will receive as much again in heaven. Neither is the parable a suggestion that the poor are sinful, but rather that barrenness after receiving God's gifts is sinful.

One of the most fascinating, and vexing, of all parables having to do with inequality is about the owner of a vineyard who hires laborers at various times of the day. Some are hired at dawn, some at midmorning, some at noon, some in midafternoon, and some just an hour before dark. He then pays them all one denarius, regardless of how many hours they worked, so that the ones who began at dawn receive only one-twelfth the hourly pay of those who began late in the day. One of the early birds complains, noting that he slaved in the hot sun wearily the entire day for the same wage that went to those who worked one cool evening hour. But the owner says, "Friend, I am doing you no wrong; did you not agree with me for a denarius? Take what belongs to you and go: I choose to give to this last as I gave to you. Am I not allowed to do what I choose with what belongs to me? Or do you begrudge me my generosity?" (Matt. 20:1)

This is obviously a difficult parable. The work ethic, then as now, assumed a relationship between pay and labor or productivity. The one who had slaved longest quite rightly expected more pay. But the master pays them all the same amount, but not at the same rate, and this "equality" is sometimes used by leftists to justify an equality of income, an "equal living wage" to each, no matter how hard he labors. But Jesus was again describing the kingdom of heaven in the parable: "For the kingdom of heaven is like a householder who went out early in the morning to hire laborers for his vineyard." He is using a worldly story to describe an otherworldly justice. The pay is equal, but the rate of pay is grossly unequal. The normal situation was for workers to receive more pay for more work, which is why the one protests. But the master rebukes him for his covetousness, pointing out that he had contracted to do a day's work for a denarius, and thus it made no difference what the others received. If they had all contracted at different rates, so what? If a man agrees of his own free will to a contract, ought he then to envy those who make better contracts? So the parable has something to do with envy, and especially the envy of those who are fortunate, who do well with little effort. Thus the parable can be used even more readily to support an antiegalitarian view. It is not a simple homily about the virtues of an equal wage. Again, it is a parable about the kingdom of heaven, where God's own mysterious justice is at work. It does suggest that God is more merciful to some than to others: his generosity to those who came last and worked least is boundless. God's contract with each person should not be subject to the envy of others.

The essence of Christian justice is not equality, but love. God's great love is forever busily evening things up in its own way, settling accounts with forgiveness and mercy. God relies on His church in the world to initiate the process, but He finishes it. The just man, in the Christian sense, is one who loves the poor and helps them, one who loves the lonely, the ill, and widows and orphans. His compassion is his justice, and he is no egalitarian scurrying through legislative chambers to divide the national income among pressure groups. His compassion does, in a way, help equalize wealth because he surrenders his own resources to those who have less, and his action is duplicated by innumerable Christians throughout society, acting individually and in concert. Thus, there is a gentle shift away from great inequalities as love begins its work. Love, in a sense, is justice, although it does not precisely allocate resources equally among those who receive it. Love is no solution for schematic social planners. Intellectuals hate it

46

because it cannot be quantified as money can. It is not a form of justice that bankers would comprehend. Despite all that, however, it is more profound than precise allocations of money, which equalize wealth but ignore human needs.

One senses in the Bible not so much an egalitarian justice as one based on fluidity of position—flux, mobility, change, God's punishments and rewards, so that indeed the last shall be first and the first shall be last—which is a scheme of events that Jesus constantly reiterates. Thus, God's justice is based on a span of time, of the evolution of events that tumble the proud and raise the humble. There is great emphasis on patience in the New Testament precisely because in time things evolve and improve. The living world is anything but static and immutable; the evil receive the fruits of their wickedness in due course. God promises that and reserves vengeance to himself. Evolution is a crucial concept of Christian justice, not only as it applies to living in the world, but in the life to come, where God compensates those who were short-changed. Indeed, much of the real meaning and purpose of faith can be found in the hope that a good God will in the end hear cries of pain and lift the poor out of their sorrows. That all takes time, however, and faith is needed to span the agony of slow-moving time.

Luke describes an incident in which Jesus, noting how eagerly some of the Jews sought positions of honor at a banquet, taught the value of humility. "When you are invited by anyone to a marriage feast," he said, "do not sit down in the place of honor lest a more eminent man than you be invited by him; and he who invited you both will come and say to you, 'Give place to this man,' and then you will begin with shame to take the lowest place. But when you are invited, go and sit in the lowest place, so when your host comes he may say to you, 'Friend go up higher': then you will be honored in the presence of all who sit at table with you. For everyone who exalts himself will be humbled, and he who humbles himself will be exalted." (Luke 14:7)

The entire lesson would make no sense in an egalitarian society, where one man is considered as good as another and where democracy is the cardinal virtue. Jesus described a natural hierarchy, a system that recognized eminence and worth, a system with places of honor, which is anything but democratic. If men were meant to be equal, then humility would be an absurd, superfluous abstraction that would accomplish nothing. In fact, humility accomplishes the recognition and honoring of worthy men; it elevates them, as the teaching so pungently points out. Here again Jesus affirms the utter diversity and inequality of men, whereas egalitarianism denies differences.

Some liberal and socialist Christians have attempted to discover a doctrinal basis for class warfare in Christianity, but none exists. In fact, Christianity is a reconciling religion that rejects any movement that would set class against class or brother against brother. To solidify the lower classes, exploit their envy, and generate a political effort to confiscate wealth, it is necessary to preach hate, to evolve myths to the effect that wealth is gathered by evil means and harsh exploitation of labor. To foster hate is to reject the central teachings of the church. On the other hand, class war by the rich is equally proscribed. To store away wealth with contempt or unconcern for workers or their families is to form a very unchristian class barrier against fellow brothers in Christ. Christianity continuously strives through time and generations for reconciliations between

47

brothers. When a poor man does not envy the rich or covet their possessions, he evokes no fear or hatred in others. When a rich man concerns himself with the welfare of the less fortunate, he evokes no hatred among the recipients of his concern. When a poor man discovers contentment in what he has and counts his blessings and thanks God for what he has, he refuses to be cannon fodder for class war. However, it is clear that Christianity places most of the burden on the rich, who are in a much better position to heal class antagonisms than the poor. A man with no money can often do little but react with rage; a man of means and power can initiate reforms and sacrifice much of what he has.

In no way did the church fathers consider the poor to be a morally superior class. There were some whose poverty was the result of sheer laziness, and these were rebuked in quite severe terms, indeed, in terms that approach the harshness of the rebukes toward the rich. Consider St. Paul on the subject:

> Now we command you, brethren . . . that you keep away from any brother who is living in idleness and not in accord with the tradition that you received from us. For you yourselves know how you ought to imitate us; we were not idle when we were with you, we did not eat anyone's bread without paying, but with toil and labor we worked day and night, that we might not burden any of you. It was not because we have not that right, but to give you in our conduct an example to imitate. For even when we were with you, we gave you this command: If any one will not work, let him not eat. For we hear that some of you are living in idleness, mere busybodies not doing any work. Now such persons we command and exhort in the Lord Jesus Christ to do their work in quietness and to earn their own living. (II Thes. 3:6)

This is a clear-cut attack on those who regard poverty as purely an environmental happenstance and who believe that all poor people are victims of capitalism or class repression. St. Paul charges Christians to work if they can; implicit in that charge is a belief in personal responsibility, an approach to life that unfortunately has been called the Protestant ethic, although it is really the Christian ethic.

Part of the reason Christians are taught to express thanks for their circumstances, no matter how miserable, is that thankfulness mitigates social antagonisms such as envy. We discover by giving thanks that we are rich in unexpected and delightful ways. Some of us are rich in health, or in perfect senses, or in the love we share with our spouse, or in the blessed goodness of our children, or in our friendships, or in the privilege of being able to work in our chosen profession, or in having a roof over our heads, or in having our own gardens. We are all rich in some ways, but none are so rich as those who have a certitude of God's love shepherding them hour by hour through life's trials. It is difficult for a Christian, sincerely grateful for all he has, to involve himself in class war or even be concerned about what the rich do with what they possess. If they buy the Hope Diamond or a famous race horse with their money, what difference is that to each of us? If we have an open heart, we learn to admire the successful and rejoice in a world that provides opportunities for all. If we wish to be forgiven, we must forgive employers, supervisors, owners, and any of the powerful who have damaged our hopes. It is not that they do us no wrong: they surely do, but out of forgiveness comes reconciliation and remedies and eventually industrial peace.

By loving both our rich and poor neighbors we begin a process of justice that is ultimately completed by God. St. James, in particular, understood the origins of class war and fiercely denounced the unjust rich who take advantage of their employees and the envious, covetous poor who rage in their hearts against the more fortunate. His object was not to eliminate classes, but to ease the antagonisms between them through Christian love. His vision was not utopian, but practical and personal; not a blueprint for a classless society, but a way to achieve peace between those with unequal status and wealth. Of course, the church, functioning in a pagan world, can achieve only so much; beyond that, justice is up to God, who alone knows who is truly rich and who is truly poor. Human envy is always based on misinformation. The envious never really grasp the sum total of misery and poverty in those they envy. When the envious do have a chance to even things up, as in the Soviet Union, it turns out that they have equalized nothing.

In the end, justice prevails because God loves all men. It is not necessary for Him to love them all equally, but rather to reward each according to his due. The process obviously begins in the life and growth of each person, so that his virtue, faith, and love have a direct impact on his happiness. Justice is a spirit of love, flowing like a river through the present.

IV

Private ownership is the principal barrier to physical equality, as socialists are well aware. If equality could be achieved without confiscating property, there would be no rationale for socialism. The root idea in all types of socialism is not public ownership, but equality. There have been numerous efforts to weld socialism to Christianity—for example, Edward Bellamy's *Looking Backward*—and in all of them Christianity has had to take the rear seat. The synthesis has always failed because both Christianity and Judaism have always jointly upheld private property and inequalities of wealth. Two of the Ten Commandments bear directly on ownership of property. The one against stealing presupposes private ownership, and the one against covetousness presupposes inequalities of wealth. Although Christian Socialism exudes an aura of benevolence toward the deprived, it actually does great violence to a wide variety of Judeo-Christian doctrine, which is why the ideology is always in the driver's seat and the faith is in the rumble seat.

Virtually the entire case for Christian Socialism rests on a single fugitive passage from Acts that describes a voluntary communism that existed briefly, and for noneconomic purposes, in the infant church:

> Now the company of those who believed were of one heart and soul, and no one said that any of the things which he possessed was his own, but they had everything in common. And with great power the apostles gave their testimony to the resurrection of the Lord Jesus, and great grace was upon them all. There was not a needy person among them, for as many as were possessors of land or houses sold them, and brought the proceeds of what was sold and laid it at the apostles' feet; and distribution was made to each as any had need. Thus Joseph

49

who was surnamed Barnabas (which means Son of encouragement) a Levite, a native of Cyprus, sold a field which belonged to him, and brought the money and laid it at the apostles' feet. (Acts 4:32)

There are several things well worth noting. (1) The communism was voluntary and thus resembled what we call Christian charity, only more so. The wealth was offered through personal volition and not garnered through government coercion. (2) This was a communism based on distribution rather than production. People sold off possessions already owned, wealth already gathered. They formed no communal industry. One assumes that, when the surplus was all sold, the communal arrangements ceased. (3) This sale permitted the apostles and others to spend full time out in the streets proselytizing the new faith rather than spend time getting an income (hence the sentence in the passage about testifying "with great power"). For a brief period, that is, the need to earn an income was suspended, and the disciples were able thereby to concentrate entirely on planting the roots of the fragile new church. Once the church was established and the communal property expended, the communal arrangement ceased. The passage also suggests that the communal life had the effect of producing intense unity and love, necessary concomitants to the freedom from work needed to establish the church. Things did return to normal; indeed, St. Paul later spent much of his ministry making and selling tents. (4) Because the surrender of wealth was voluntary, it did not violate the commandment against stealing. (5) Finally, because the commune did not produce, but only distributed, it did not violate the Mosaic laws guaranteeing that the worker shall have a right to the fruits of his labor. St. Paul elaborated on this ancient right in I Corinthians 9: "Who serves as a soldier at his own expense? Who plants a vineyard without eating any of its fruit? Who tends a flock without getting some of the milk? Do I say all this on human authority? Does not the law say the same? For it is written in the law of Moses, 'You shall not muzzle an ox when it is treading the grain.' Is it for the oxen that God is concerned? Does he not speak entirely for our own sake? It was written for our sake because the plowman should plow in hope and the thresher thresh in hope of a share of the crop."

Obviously, this early, brief Christian communism differs sharply with modern state socialism. It existed to free the early church apostles for a time, whereas modern socialism exists for an economic purpose, to equalize wealth. It was voluntary, taking nothing by force, and it operated without reference to the state or its taxing power. It was not organized for production, although socialism is organized to produce, as well as distribute, through publicly owned enterprises. It did not sever the crucial relationship between effort and reward, between work and payment, whereas socialism is based on an equality of income, no matter how hard anyone works. Thus, in a variety of ways the early commune was not comparable to socialism, and had quite opposite goals— spiritual rather than material. It was an expression of Christian love rather than pagan envy. Men learned new dimensions of fraternity and charity from the experience and were thereby bonded together so strongly that not all the efforts of the rulers of Judea to pry them apart succeeded.

Modern socialism, on the other hand, builds no bridges between hearts. An abstract responsibility is substituted for love. Those who receive acquire their due as a matter of legal right, coldly and impersonally. They need feel no gratitude for the mechanical dole, and they rarely do. Least of all do they feel grateful to those whose labor or genius contributed to their dole. Modern socialism does not reconcile men or change souls or warm hearts; if anything, it hardens hearts and develops a callousness among men. Christian socialists evade the stark differences between their blueprints and the gentle commune of the Jerusalem Christians, and by evading those differences they end up worshiping at the altar of statism.

If private ownership were not the basis for all the social arrangements implicit in Christianity, many of the teachings of the church would lack meaning. Under the reign of pure democracy or absolute equality, what would be the sense of encouraging charity, hope, or humility? Why bother with problems of stealing and covetousness? There would be no rich, hence no reason to warn them of their special obligations. There would be no point in denouncing envy if no one had anything enviable. In other words, why does the church take the roundabout method of mitigating inequalities through love, charity, and a sense of obligation when it could take the direct approach and advocate universal socialism? Socialism, after all, would theoretically eliminate the need for most Christian virtues. The answer is that private ownership is fundamental to the whole system of Christianity. Without private ownership, its teachings make no sense.

Surely, if Jesus Christ had perceived that a system of state-run socialism would resolve man's most agonizing problems, He would have advocated it directly. He would have spoken bluntly and plainly about it, as He did about other moral and ethical precepts. He would have denounced ownership as inherently evil. He would have asserted that property divides brothers and prevents love. He would have insisted that inequalities were the root of all evil. He said nothing of the sort, which is why it is so perverse to attach a socialist doctrine to Christianity. The value system He taught is expressly applicable to private ownership with varying degrees of affluence and poverty. There are, of course, Christian virtues such as faith and obedience that have little to do with private ownership. But the Christian and Jewish ethical system, which supports unequal ownership, the validity of contract, and the concept of a free will that can be exercized responsibly, rests squarely on man's natural impulse to gather his own possessions around him. The Communists are perfectly honest about the irreconcilability of Christian religion with their system; the socialists are less honest and keep hoping at least to derive an ethic common to socialism and Christianity. The Liberals are not so much dishonest as muddled: frequently they profess a sincere Christianity while promoting the sort of egalitarianism the faith rejects. I have great difficulty understanding how anyone can claim to be both a leftist and a Christian.

V

The quest for equality is the quest for death. Indeed, only in death does equality among men reign at last. Only when bodies and minds cease to function in all their marvelous diversity is everything finally leveled to a common plane. Some, indeed, are buried in splendid mausoleums, while others lie in potter's fields— a last, desperate thrust toward inequality—but once physical life has ceased, there are no fortunate or unfortunate, rich or poor, healthy or sick, rulers or ruled.

The achievement of equality rests on the social ability to deaden life. The most robust, vital, vibrant peoples are precisely those among whom natural inequalities and imbalances flourish, among whom status and wealth approximate the spread of industry, courage, and intelligence. The closer a society approaches an enforced equality, the more it ravages the virtues, hopes, dreams, faith, and patriotism of its citizens. In a society that guarantees that one's income will always remain in step with those of others, all human aspirations of an economic nature are denied meaning. A man's industry will get him nowhere. A man's prudence, perseverance, and wisdom will avail him almost nothing. Conversely, laziness, improvidence, or an unruly temper carry no grave penalties. Employment itself could scarcely have value, except to stave off boredom, so long as income is guaranteed. Inventiveness, authorship, entrepreneurial skill would have only spiritual rewards. So one sees death rattling through all the egalitarian communities, especially communist societies, where the only pockets of life and vitality are to be found where inequalities flourish. It is true that when men work for the advancement of the "state" or the "proletariat" or the "people," they see some benefits ultimately redounding to themselves, but there is no particular sense of personal progress, no personal plans or goals of consequence, and most of life is an enervating drift through the twilight zone. The name of the Grim Reaper is Equality.

Only a rare man can subsume all his energies and yearnings, his innate industriousness and eagerness to advance to such an abstract goal as "the people." The mass of men, when forced to serve such a rarefied ideal, sink into a vegetative life until they reach mere subsistence levels. The professed egalitarian regimes are then forced to reinstate pockets of privilege and ownership to provide incentives: small plots of land for peasants on the big collectives; high salaries and prestige for the scientific-technological community; or the privileges of party membership for the ruling elite. Immediately, when privileges and inequalities are introduced, life blossoms, energies are deployed, and vitalities are to a degree restored.

If it is true that man does not live by bread alone, it is equally true that he does not live by spirit alone. Christianity has placed great emphasis on the spiritual and material duality of man and unfortunately too little stress on the unity of the person. A large portion of the ministry of Jesus was devoted to healing bodies, but that healing was almost always connected with healing the spirit. Thus, he told people whose bodies he mended that their sins were forgiven, and he urged them to repent. He understood that an unclean or broken spirit had its deadly effect on the body; he understood the unity of persons. The egalitarian society inflicts as much death on bodies as upon souls: it destroys man's spiritual growth as much as it destroys his economic hopes and well-being.

The first fruits of a rigid egalitarianism are not brotherhood and fraternity, but dwindling concern for others and a horrifying, icy isolation. It is a rare man

52

in the Soviet Union who dares to bare his soul, an equally rare man who dares to listen to another victim of the workers' paradise bare his soul. Loneliness and lovelessness are the most crushing burdens carried by the victims of totalitarianism. They can bear economic hardship, they can bear the disappearance of liberty, but it is almost impossible for them to bear their load of isolation. With the gradual shift of Soviet children away from families, where there are too many inequalities, and into public boarding schools, the regime will eventually smash the last little islands of love and companionship and then will leave each of the citizens of that fortunate paradise splendidly isolated. So the virtues die, and equality crucifies men, women, and children without regard to race, creed, national origin, or previous condition of servitude. Equality is perhaps the exact synonym for hell. The extent to which societies manage to equalize men is the extent of their senility, the index of their decline, the mark of a terminal disease.

Jesus prophesied that in the last days the love of many would grow cold, a prophecy that may have been based on His knowledge of the impact of egalitarianism. For on the heels of ideological equality comes the death of love and thus the death of man's most meaningful and sublime experience. Love does not seek to make every man equal, but seeks the fulfillment of each. Love does not wish damnation upon the rich, and nothing is quite so alien to love as that mathematical envy that measures distances from one man to the next. We do no favor to any man by wishing equality on him. Each is too complex for such a simple formula. Rather, we hope each person can develop his best talents, overcome his worst weaknesses, discover a daily joy in existing circumstances, achieve material comfort consonant with his needs, and learn to transcend the world. If we can love, we can wish that upon each person, regardless of his sex or color.

Equality is ultimately nihilistic because it negates values. For example, when egalitarian passions are applied to education, the result is the demolition of excellence. We see the democratic passion at work everywhere: grades and examinations are eliminated, and thus the measurements of learning are pitched out. Pass-fail systems are installed so every student can feel "equal" to the rest. Grading systems are "bent" to accommodate the "deprived." A committee of the English Labour Party argues that examinations "at present exert a disproportionate influence in the curriculum and tend to be inflexible and irrelevant to the world today as well as *reinforcing social divisions.*"[1] Competitive games are abolished so that there may be no victors and losers and no little psyche hurt by failure. Thus are academic standards wantonly slaughtered and inequalities tabooed. Huge sums are spent for remedial education for the disadvantaged with emotional problems or low intelligence to make them "equal," but nothing of consequence is spent on bright children to help them become unequal. It is not "democratic" to help the bright and aggressive to achieve their potentials. Thus, equality has a nihilistic impact on education, attacking the very meaning and rationale for imparting information

---

[1] Quoted by C. B. Cox, *Papers on Educational Reform,* III; LaSalle, Ill.: Open Court Pub. Co., 1973. Italics added.

and wisdom to the young. Death stalks the academies, and the name of death is Equality.

A similar nihilism undergirds a whole branch of psychology and anthropology. The behaviorist psychology is rooted in an egalitarian approach to mankind: people are all equally mechanisms, responding reflexively to environmental stimulants. Thus inequalities are interpreted as the result of environment, social milieu, climate, or luck. Wherever unfavorable stimulants, such as a loveless mother, an illiterate family, or poverty had an impact on those little equal machines called children, their growth was stunted. By contrast, wherever the little machines were given love, a literate home, and educated parents, the little machines flourished. The whole system is as clear as the twitches of Pavlov's dog. So the behaviorists suggest that free will and liberty are illusions, or worse, delusions. The environment is Big Brother. All men are equal; only environments are unfair and impose their inequity on the human species.

Obviously, there is some validity to some of the behavioral ideas. We do respond to our environments; we do in fact develop a dynamic relation to the world around us, imposing our will on it, transforming it, even as we are shaped by it, through constant exchanges of energy and will and determination. Moreover, behaviorism has clinical applications and has been used successfully to correct psychopathic behavior by punishing the destructive and rewarding the creative aspects of confused personalities. One of the main sources of mental disease is the rewarding of evil behavior by misapplying love and neglecting to punish. Behaviorism nevertheless has deep and ominous social implications because it fundamentally denies that men are different and insists that we begin as alike as field mice. The behaviorist sees even our will and our industry as fairly simple mechanical responses to our environment. It is not a free will, but a conditioned will; the will that appears freer than others was merely one conditioned to dominate environment better than others. It is all a matter of equality and of mechanics: stimulus and response.

The whole theory does violence to the capability and spirit and genius of mankind. It cannot really explain his strange valor; his willingness to martyr himself on occasion; his logical capacity; his rationality; his intuitions; his quest to dominate; the diversity of his interests; in short, his glory and diversity. Behaviorism ultimately cannot explain Martin Luther or Jeanne d' Arc or St. Benedict. Neither can it explain miracles, the things that happen through pure faith. To reduce man to a set of reflexes, to deny his humanity and will is to make him a cipher, to annihilate him and negate him, to make him a mere ape. If he is an ape, made unequal merely by the impact of circumstance, then there is a rationality in the effort to equalize all environmental circumstances. It is no wonder that the New Left is infatuated with behaviorist thought, which denies all personality, affirms total equality, and pins the entire blame on evil institutions and circumstances that must be reformed or at least torn down.

It is true, of course, that all this is somewhat of a simplification of behaviorist doctrine, designed to elucidate its underlying egalitarian nihilism.

Behaviorists do, to a degree, admit to minor variations in the human machine, variations that have to do with metabolism or body dysfunctions. For all its nuances and occasional concessions to heredity, however, it remains a radically nihilist and egalitarian doctrine of psychology, and it does not shrink from its own logical imperative that man's institutions must be radically reformed so that human machines can develop equally. For that reason, its chief apostle, B. F. Skinner, is a darling of the left.

Behaviorism, needless to say, is totally at odds with Christian thought, which affirms free will, personal autonomy, and the capacity of men, who are made in God's image, to have responsible dominion over the environment. It assumes that they are capable of moral choice through their free will, have a knowledge of good and evil, are capable of modifying their own behavior through their own will, and have a creativity that can transcend learning or environment. Where Christianity builds a concept of personhood, of an intelligence functioning in the image of God, an intelligence that transcends mere stimuli, behaviorism reduces this belief, denies free will and responsibility, and reduces man to a cipher. No serious behaviorist could ever reconcile his ideology with Christianity: his membership in a Christian church would be an act of wanton hypocrisy.

The democratic quest for equality is also responsible for the folly of cultural relativism, the notion that one society is the equal of any other because there are no objective standards by which civilizations can be measured, no way to determine superiority or inferiority. Societies are regarded as mere adaptations to the local milieu; if a bushman survives comfortably on a diet of raw lizards, who is to say that his lot is any worse than that of the man whose food comes in an infinite variety from groceries that are the end result of a system that collects foods from the far ends of the globe and brings them to the consumer undamaged and unspoiled? The lunacy of such cultural egalitarianism is obvious from the standpoint of simple common sense, but it still attracts certain obsessed intellectuals of the left who are eager to equate any vice in Western society with a similar vice in a Stone Age culture. The current rage is to extol the American Indian cultures as innately equal or even superior to the European because they achieved some harmony with nature, did little ecological damage, and did not squander resources. This warped theory ignores the hardship, the cold, and the virtual starvation that generally plagued the Indians. It ignores their bloody tribal warfare, their torture, their primitive superstitions, their incapacity to multiply beyond a few million even though they had a rich continent open to them and no foreign culture to stop them. It is a theory concocted by egalitarian intellectuals who sit in comfortable armchairs in heated houses, enjoying all the advances of medicine and production and science, intellectuals who would quickly perish if forced to live in animal-skin tents on the open plains, constantly fighting off nature, hostile Indians, and disease.

It is true that the Indians left nature relatively intact, but also true that they lived miserably, improvidently, barbarously, and never very far from disaster. Few among them, except for the Pueblos in the Southwest, planted and harvested or stored food, or practiced livestock husbandry, or lived settled lives.

They even lacked the wheel and metals. In short, the sort of cultural egalitarianism that extols their life is a masochism of the civilized, practiced to perfection by white leftists with white guilt complexes, men who are desperately afraid that Western civilization really is superior, hence unequal. It is not even true that the Indians conserved nature. Their practice of stampeding entire buffalo herds over a cliff, killing far more than they could use or store for the future, is scarcely an example of conservation. Still, the intellectuals are quick to condemn only the white buffalo hunters. Surely the intellectual impulse to reduce Western Christian culture to the level of the tribalism elsewhere in the world is nihilism, a simple denial of all standards of sophistication and superiority for the sake of equality. It is, in a sense, an attack on God, an assault on the universe God made.

VI

There is a liberalistic notion abroad that society need not be strictly equal so long as all children entering into it are given an equal opportunity. The idea is to line up everyone at the same starting line and then let each run as far and as fast as he can, fulfilling all his potentialities, so that the end result would indeed reflect the unequal abilities of each. The idea is absurd. It ignores the fact that generations overlap. A man who lives his three score years and ten can expect to know his children for perhaps 50 of those years, and his grandchildren as well. If we were all bugs that laid our eggs in the fall and died, so that the new generation in the spring would have an equal start, equally disinherited, there would be some resemblance of equality, provided that all bugs were genetic equals and had exactly the same access to shelter, climate, and food.

Our generations overlap, however, and if we let all men run as far and as fast as they can, they will transmit their advantages and liabilities to their offspring. The children of a genius whose inventions earn millions will have a different starting line from those of a neurotic who cannot keep a job or learn to be productive. He who advocates an equal starting line is, therefore, really advocating a rigid system of equality that lets no man rise above others at any time in life, a system that must paralyze the genius and reward the neurotic. The radically leftist and communist states recognize that family life is the crux of the problem because families foster advantage or disadvantage through the generations. Hence the effort in the Red world to pluck children from their parents and stuff them into state boarding schools where they will be compelled to live in physically equal environments, or line up at the "same starting line in life," always assuming that all the schools are equal and that no subversive teacher inspires the students to greatness. In the less socialistic and more liberal cultures, the egalitarians content themselves with opposing private and parochial schools, especially the endowed academies, lest someone, somewhere, be brilliantly educated, guilty of the horrendous sin of excellence, which leads to the even more abhorrent sin of inequality, or even aristocracy!

The equal-starting-line notion is foiled beyond repair by genetic as well as environmental differences: not merely by intelligence, but also by emotional life, reaction to heat and cold and pain, the perfection of such senses as sight and hearing, allergies, stamina, metabolism, size, beauty or plainness, all of which bear directly on whether little Johnnie or Susie will be ahead or behind the pack from the start. Not until we achieve test-tube reproduction and positive control of genes that can combine into infinite diversity—that is, not until the state and science conspire to plunge us into a monstrous invasion of God's prerogatives—can there be a genetic leveling. When it comes, it will be the dreariest civilization, as well as the stupidest, ever conceived. But count on man to try it, with all the enthusiasm the intellectuals can muster for the true key to egalitarianism.

The notion of lining up all the youngsters on the same starting line by regulating parental income is absurd. The family with a command of language, a lively interest in ideas, good books at every hand, natural curiosity, and hospitality toward others who profess differing views will contribute to the superiority of its progeny even if its income is quite sparse, or even identical to the penny with that of its less bright neighbors who watch TV all day while piling through the sixpacks.

There is even an effort to compel rich school districts to subsidize poor ones, all in the name of equality. The theory is that the districts with less expenditure per pupil are denying their children the "equal protection of the law" that has become so sacred to egalitarians. Current evidence suggests that excellence in education has little to do with expenditures per pupil, or teacher loading, or classroom size, or counseling, or such frills as swimming pools. All the evidence points to family life as the main environmental determinant. Moreover, districts that have bought and paid for fine facilities may well have a lower expenditure per pupil than those districts that are in debt or are spending a great deal for a mediocre system.

The nonsense of the equal starting line crops up constantly in leftist literature and thinking. One cannot comprehend what good would be achieved by the success of the scheme, unless by some miracle it functioned at the highest, rather than the lowest, common denominator. As things stand now, the equalizer must balance his concern for the deprived with a resentment of the fortunate. The result is morally dubious. To destroy the good fortune of a rich child or to deprive a brilliant child of the chance to plunge ahead, all in the name of equality, is to make them the disinherited, the deprived, the cheated. It is a basic Christian virtue to proceed through life without reference to the status of neighbors, loving all as far as possible, without respect for persons.

If we take all types of poverty and all types of riches into account, there is much more justice in the world than egalitarians wish to admit. One senses a loving God always at work, overturning things, elevating and lowering people and groups and societies, shifting and mixing all mankind in a manner that continually brings new facets of love and joy and life to each. Each of the children of the world has immense riches as well as deprivations residing within him. A very rich tycoon may have no appreciation for music or art. A cerebral intellectual may be impoverished by an inability to dance. A poet with aesthetic riches may lack business sense. A poor man may find riches in a walk in the woods. An idiot may well find life as enchanting as a children's fairy story. An affluent lady may be chronically ill. A rich child may be hopelessly lazy. A great mathematician may be helpless to express himself. One senses that men who are first in one realm are last in another; that God's promise that the first shall be last and the last shall be first is a dynamic that is occurring all the time through life and history in a variety of ways. Few men are king of the mountain for long. No man is rich in every realm of his existence. Justice is everywhere at hand: one thinks, for example, of the economist John Kenneth Galbraith, whose Olympian height is perhaps a great consolation for his intellectual shortcomings. Poverty and wealth are rolled up into one speck of humanity. So justice does prevail in a continuing way: the Lord giveth and the Lord taketh away. The poor and rich each have pleasures and burdens, and if worldly life is harder for the poor, there will be compensations at the end. When crisis turns the world upside down, the privileged and protected, who lack the ability to survive, suffer and die, while the Admirable Crightons become lords of the species, flourishing where more civilized men die off. It is grotesque to suppose that equalizing income or opportunity can really redistribute happiness or equalize misery when, in the larger sense, there exists already a fairly even distribution of pleasure and sorrow among most men. It is, in a sense, superfluous: God has arranged the world so that happiness is available to all who seek it.

There is, moreover, a constant flux, an evolution that is a major theme of biblical teachings about justice. The net effect of motion is to produce a certain type of equality not describable as physical leveling, but as a means of giving each his due. God's promises are filled not only in heaven, but in time. If that were not true, patience would scarcely be a Christian virtue, and hope would have no meaning. Some of that motion is social mobility. The poor clamber up the ladders, while the foolish or unfortunate among the rich topple down. One sees evidence of it at every hand: wastrels demolishing family fortunes, while the denizens of hell catapult ahead. Even Hell's Kitchen has its honor roll. The boy whose intellectual development is stunted because of a poor school system may become a brilliant baseball player or boxer. The bored student with a little money in his jeans may throw away a fine future and numb himself with pot, which like alcohol, is an escape from the pain of living and struggling and therefore an agent of spiritual death. Time is the essence of all this mobility; time is what demolishes a lazy genius unwilling to suffer in order to produce; time is what rewards a plodder who has the courage to keep trying until he succeeds. The tale of the tortoise and the hare is the story of God's own version of equality at work, or rather God's love, which rewards good and constant effort. To the extent that socialism imposes its man-made equality and "justice" on men, it impedes this great mobility that is God's way of giving each his due. Socialism is a rebellion against God's way of ordering His universe.

If all this is true, then those who seek to squash men to fit their own vision of utopia—I am speaking of all leftists—are impeding God's great justice. The levelers are the enemies of the natural order, inciting envy in some, guillotining others, taxing still others, and in the end only preventing God's will from being done on earth as it is in heaven.

When we consider the infinite ways in which a man can be poor or rich, we can only conclude that it would be arrogant or presumptuous to invade God's sovereignty with a scheme such as socialism or liberalism. It is one thing to be charitable, to help a suffering man whose skin is dark, to help a woman change a tire, or to invite an old bachelor to dinner. It is quite another to level the whole race. To imagine that any "ism" can achieve justice, can equalize happiness, so to speak, is simply idolatry. Communism is the most notorious secular religion, but the American version of liberalism has the same weird grip on this nation's elite. There are too many variables at work for planners and blueprinters to comprehend, variables that end up cheating the bulk of men of whatever joy they might have had in a freer society. Only God knows how worthy we are; how each of us responded to trouble and difficulty; how we grew; how we evaded responsibilities; how we secretly rewarded ourselves; how we waited patiently for his flux to work in time; how faithful we were. We can perceive ultimate justice only in God's terms, a justice infinitely greater than all the computers of man, harnessed together, could even begin to quantify.

3

No Womb at the Top

I

At times I think it would be best for women alone to evaluate the new feminism. A man is likely to be unfair. If I do it, I must reach through the glass and gauze that divides the sexes, and I am uncertain that I can do so. I cannot envision Gloria Steinem as she would want me to: she strikes me as passably attractive, with those huge eyeshades, and I suppose that would please her not one bit. So I cannot hope to assess the Liberation from the vantage point that Lib would prefer. I am not certain, in any case, that my assessment would suffer on that account. If I write from a male viewpoint, does that disqualify me, ipso facto? No. If one can write discerningly about, say, the Communists without being one, then surely one can write discerningly about Lib without being female.

I stake my claim on that ground. Moreover, since Lib ideology has cast men as devils, I claim the right to remove my horns; to do less would be a forfeit. In any case, I am not at war with the other sex, although some men are—Norman Mailer, for instance. In recent months he mounted a considerable assault on Lib,[1] but in my estimation it was to little avail. Poor Mailer was never able to hack his way out of the genital jungles and thus was never able to perceive women as whole personalities with spiritual, social, emotional, and vocational facets to their personalities. He managed a page or two about the impoverishment of women by capitalist robbers, but these paragraphs taste like cold spinach, and he was obviously out of his element until he returned to his pubic forests. He did, however, manage one small ambush on the freeway to defeat: he proved beyond doubt that the Lib ideologists are intellectual gangsters, bilking the goddess of truth.

[1] Norman Mailer, *The Prisoner of Sex*. Boston: Little, Brown & Co., 1971.

Mailer's most telling blows landed on Kate Millett, whose *Sexual Politics* is one of the Lib gospels. Miss Millett had set out to prove, among other things, a contempt for women in the writings of D. H. Lawrence and Henry Miller—a not implausible theory. However, she plundered the passages so recklessly that Mailer had only to shoot point blank to drop that bird. He also got some buckshot into Greer and Friedan, but they survived, even if Lib's reputation for scholarship will never be the same.

My own modest researches have led me to the same conclusion. Lib is distorting reality to establish its thesis that 50 percent of the human race is oppressed. It does not matter in any militant enterprise whether its devils are real or imagined, only that they are believable. It is apparent even to a casual sojourner in Libland that women have erected formidable devils and that these devils wear trousers, as I do. Male chauvinist pigs have allegedly connived from time immemorial to subjugate women and deny them their rights, their humanity, and the fruits of their labor. It is all amazing, and I deny the charge.

In some ways, I suppose, I'm a fellow traveller, willing to concede the validity of some Lib goals, such as equal pay for equal work, even while I frown on Lib methods. For example, I am tempted to accept the women's rights amendment now going the rounds of the legislatures. It would wipe out a mass of bad law based on sexual considerations and would even things up for dukes and duchesses. Particularly in the realm of labor legislation it would be a good, cathartic thing to free women from the "protections" that impede their economic advancement. As a libertarian, I am aware that such protection usually swindles people out of an adequate income.

Opponents of the amendment dread its impact on laws protecting family life, but I am convinced that the amendment could actually strengthen families if state legislatures reenacted the nullified laws, making the rights and obligations reciprocal for both sexes. One can examine the whole gaggle of law designed to fortify family life and conclude that legal reciprocity, or equality, would quickly lower the divorce rate and materially reduce the impulse of women to shed their husbands. At present, women have nothing to lose: they can dump their husbands and still end up with the children, child-support payments, alimony, and a house, while ex-husbands are dealt involuntary servitude and grinding loneliness, if not poverty. Under the equality amendment, women would have as much or more to lose, and that might improve the prospects for reconciliation. The present law literally invites women to sue; their life can continue intact, after a divorce, except for a husband.

If I oppose the amendment, however, it is basically because I think women are different. They need rights and laws and privileges of their own and not merely an abstract theoretic equality with men. Under an equality amendment, for example, there could be no such thing as maternity leave: a woman who leaves employment to have a child could not, in many instances, protect her job. Justice is better served by legislation that provides for the biological imperatives of her sex. I really do not believe that women should be fighting wars, for example, but the thrust of the amendment would compel women, not only to be in the armed services, but to be in the front lines, in combat units, on an equal basis with their male peers. As far as women are concerned, my general attitude is "Vive la différence!"

So then: I place myself on the side of the Libbers—to a degree. I am inclined to say about them, as was once said so piously about Joe McCarthy, "I approve of their goals, but despise their methods." That, of course, is not really true, because I scarcely approve of abortions on demand or Federal child care centers. Moreover, Libbers are more intransigent and less scrupulous than Joe McCarthy and thus approachable only gingerly, gingerly. If the Libbers—I firmly separate them from other women—ever grab the helm, I expect to have my neck severed by those knitting furies or find myself hauled up before a Congressional committee on grounds of aiding and abetting a secret sexist conspiracy.

At any rate, the best way to assess the legitimacy of Lib ideology is to probe into its truthfulness. If it is true that women have been historically subjugated in cruel and numbing ways; if it is true that they have been doomed to child-bearing and have been denied freedom, property, and education; if it is all true, then the grievances are legitimate, and reform is surely welcome. On the other hand, if the feminists are peddling mostly hokum, then the enterprise should be stuffed out the window.

I confess that, prior to the rise of Lib, I had prejudices that did not accord with what the feminists are saying. I had supposed that we were living in the Golden Age of women—an epoch almost miraculous in terms of opportunity, health, and diversity for the allegedly gentle sex. I had supposed that women are enjoying minimal drudgery, maximum variety, and considerably better health and longevity than men. There were wondrous innovations to lighten housework, prepackage meals, minimize diaper problems, and simplify shopping. There seemed to be time for women to enjoy leisure: to fulfill the dream of all mankind to have the time to cultivate one's mind, to join pro bono groups, to pursue arts and belles lettres, to engage in charity, hospital service, and welfare. I had heard that women owned most of the nation's wealth and spent most of the family budget, thus powerfully shaping its tastes and style of living. Beyond the leisurely family life there was always the prospect of frequent travel and careers, somewhat more limited than men's, but nonetheless as broad and open as talent could command. I had further supposed that, if any sex was in trouble, it was the male. Men had become bumbling, servile incompetents in too many cases, working at drudgery for a lifetime to keep their wives wrapped in ermine and whiling away the sweaty summers at the office while their wives toured Europe or fled to cool lake cottages. Any female discontents I ascribed mainly to boredom, with which I do not sympathize because it is usually the fault of the bored. The most discontented women, I supposed, were those whose victory over the male sex was too total, who had abraded their husbands into submission, who had come to dominate their men, children, and friends so relentlessly that self-hatred clawed at their innards because their position had become unnatural.

Ever so reluctantly, I have been forced to retreat from that assessment. Lib literature conveyed quite another picture, in which women were forever the second sex, or maybe the third, barefoot, ill-paid, servile, oppressed, sexually abused, imprisoned, forced to be passive, and denied education. I have never been able to surrender my prejudices entirely, but Lib literature has surely stressed the ambiguity and variety of women's roles in our culture. Women are simultaneously weak and powerful; rich and denied economic opportunity; free for astounding leisure and loaded with drudgery; denied vocational choice, but free to pursue the wildest dreams of most males.

So far as the feminists are concerned, my theory of the Golden Age is pure sexism, the conceit of a male chauvinist. Their entire ideology—and it is an ideology, blossoming full-blown in a few years of incubation—assumes that women are strictly a persecuted class, similar to other classes such as the blacks or the proletariat. The biological reality of motherhood had nothing to do with it: the womb was merely the male rationalization for a slavery that was really economic in its underpinnings. Ultimately, however, this Lib ideology poses a false dilemma: either a woman must be a domestic drudge and sex slave or she must become a liberated, male-hating career type with no moral strings on her sex life. In between there is only the prickly porcupine business of Lib-style marriage, with its mathematical allocations of child care and dishwashing and meal cooking; an armed camp in which there is no joy in assuming any of the work load; a marriage held together by treaties rather than a mature happiness in pitching in to get things done. The dilemma is unreal, and it reflects the shabby scholarship undergirding the Lib *putsch*. This commentary will be concerned mainly with establishing a better picture of women's status in the United States, with a discussion of the real options that actual, not mythological, women enjoy, so that the horns of the Lib dilemma will prove to be less sharp than the ladies suppose. Before we dig deep into the status of modern women, it will be necessary to go back to the roots of Western Civilization and see what Christianity, the church fathers in particular, had to say about the status and obligations of women.

II

The sorities sisters are convinced that Christianity, or perhaps the Judeo-Christian tradition, has done them in. Indeed, the assault on sex roles established in the Old and New Testaments is the centerpiece of the whole Lib criticism of the European and North American value system. Christian scripture does in fact define two areas in which men are vested with primary authority. One is marriage and the other is church administration. Both Saints Peter and Paul have things to say about the primacy of husbands in marriage, and Paul has much to say about male authority in conducting the business of the church, including worship. However, that authority is clearly limited; women are joint heirs to the kingdom of heaven, and women are welcome on equal terms with men in nearly every aspect of Christian life, including proselytizing and teaching. The only assumption of inequality I have been able to discern is the belief that women are physically weaker and perhaps more talkative. There is no assumption that women are an inferior sex or lack male intelligence or lack the ability to form good character. Neither is there an assumption that women must be confined to servant-helper status or domestic drudgery.

It is possible, however, for Lib ideologues to build a case that Christianity is sexist by lifting certain verses of Scripture out of context. For that reason, a leisurely examination of women's situations throughout the New Testament is worthwhile, and a glance at the Old Testament is equally helpful. The entire Jewish and Christian ethic must also be considered in the context of the tendency in the ancient world to treat women as chattels or mere sex objects. It is quite possible that so many pagan or gentile women, such as Priscilla, flocked to the new religion of Jesus of Nazareth because they discovered for the first time in their lives that they could be full partners in grace and life and not simply the chief domestics in the households of men of that waning epoch.

The four gospels scarcely mention Jesus' attitude toward women, and that in itself is significant because it weakens any claims that one sex was treated better by the Lord than the other. We do know that throughout his brief ministry he was surrounded by numbers of women, especially the Marys and Marthas. It is true that his disciples were men, but so was the Jewish priesthood. It is also true that women seemed to be always at hand and are mentioned frequently through the gospels. Women, too, were the first to receive the news of the resurrection at the tomb. One incident, recorded by Luke, should give joy to any woman who wonders about her status within the faith. Luke records that Jesus visited the home of two sisters, Martha and Mary: ". . . he entered the village; and a woman named Martha received him into her house. She had a sister called Mary, who sat at the Lord's feet and listened to his teaching. But Martha was distracted with much serving; and she went to him and said, 'Lord, do you not care that my sister has left me to serve alone? Tell her then to help me.' But the Lord answered her, 'Martha, Martha, you are anxious and troubled about many things: one thing is needful. Mary has chosen the good portion which shall not be taken away from her.' " (Luke 10: 38 RSV)

Thus in one happy moment he affirmed Mary's right to the "good portion," that is, to her education, and indeed to her right to set aside domestic labor when more important things are at hand. We are not told exactly what one thing was needful, but we may assume it had to do with Martha's anxiety about unimportant things, such as serving, an anxiety that she should set aside to receive the "good portion." This invitation to obtain an education, to seek knowledge in the house of intellect, was a poignant honor in an era when the rabbinical traditional centered strongly on the male sex. The incident was typical of him and was a good example of the way He imparted his love to all around him.

St. Paul bears the brunt of the Lib criticism of Christian "sexism," no doubt because he was informed by the strict pharisaical code of male authority in religious and domestic institutions. It should be borne in mind that the Christian definition of authority is essentially one of service to others, of a ministry, epitomized by the episode in which Jesus washed the feet of his disciples, admonishing them to seek greatness in that fashion. Moreover, authority is not the same as superiority. We vest authority in our governors because someone must govern and not necessarily because the governors are superior in most ways to the rest of us.

St. Paul's harshest strictures upon women are found in his first letter to the

Corinthians, in which he wrote that "women should keep silence in the churches. For they are not permitted to speak, but should be subordinate as even the law says. If there is anything they desire to know, let them ask their husbands at home. For it is shameful for a woman to speak in the church. What? did the word of God originate with you or are you the only ones it has reached?" (14:34)

Here Paul evokes the Jewish law, but in Galatians he affirms the complete equality of women in the Church of Christ: "There is neither Jew nor Greek, there is neither slave nor free, there is neither male nor female: for you are all one in Christ Jesus." (Gal. 3:28) Thus, whatever he may have felt about what the Jewish law ordained in worship, he bluntly made it clear that no class or caste need feel inferior or superior before God. While he expected women to fall under male authority in the work of the church, he surely considered women full partners in grace. It is doubtful that Paul was as adamant about women's silence during worship as his letters suggest. At least, there is a passage in Corinthians, devoted to such minutiae as covering of heads, in which he asserts that it is shameful for a woman not to have her head covered while praying or prophesying, which are activities that may involve speaking up during worship. Paul's alleged misogyny really boils down to some strong ideas about fitness of conduct in church, a subject to which we will shortly return.

Peter shared Paul's certitude about the universality of grace. He urged husbands to "live considerately with your wives, bestowing honor on the woman as the weaker sex, since you are joint heirs of the grace of life. . . ." If women are the joint heirs, then they are on the same equal terms with God as the men, no matter how they stand in respect to church authority.

In Paul's theology, women lost their right to church authority when Eve yielded to the serpent. In his first letter to Timothy he explains: "Let a woman learn in silence with all submissiveness. I permit no woman to teach or to have authority over men; she is to keep silent. For Adam was formed first, then Eve; and Adam was not deceived, but the woman was deceived and became a transgressor. Yet woman will be saved through bearing children, if she continues in faith and love and holiness, with modesty." (I Tim. 2:11)

Paul's version of the fall is scarcely fair or accurate, because Adam also ate the fruit handed him by Eve, and worse, ate it knowingly, undeceived. Elsewhere, also, in Rom. 5:12, Paul blames Adam for the fall. The curse God imposes on Eve is severe: "She shall know the pain of childbirth, and her husband shall rule over her." But the curse God imposes on Adam is much worse, indeed formidable: "Cursed is the ground because of you; thorns and thistles it shall bring forth to you; and you shall eat the plants of the field. In the sweat of your face you shall eat bread till you return to the ground. . . ." No matter whether the story is allegorical or literal, the dual curses of God have structured the sex roles as we know them to this day throughout all Christendom. Men work by the sweat of their face and normally head households; women suffer the agony of childbirth and are usually not the heads of households.

I prefer to remember the loving sweep of God's concern for us all, and that is why I think the Pauline strictures are relatively unimportant. In no Christian tradition do they occupy anything like the center of faith. God is surely not sexist in the sense that he loves one sex more and the other less. Scripture is laden with both ambiguity and contradiction, which forces some fundamentalists to attempt desperate reconciliations of conflicting passages on the assumption that such imperfections are impossible in the World of God. Such efforts only addle the mind and, worse, draw attention away from the true thrust of the scriptures. The mind boggles at the contortions of those who have set out to reconcile the lusty temperaments of the apostles. It is perfectly possible to discover the Word of God at the center, even if the apostles' details vary according to their recollections and temperaments. A real test of faith is to discover Truth within the conflicting scriptures, to see the Holy Spirit at work in such diverse minds as Paul's and Peter's and John's.

Paul was not a misogynist, full of venom toward women. Neither did he conceive of women as mere childbearing creatures. Consider his description of Christian marriage, found in his letter to the Ephesians: "Wives, be subject to your husbands, as to the Lord. For the husband is the head of the wife as Christ is the head of the church, his body, and is himself its savior. . . . Husbands love your wives as Christ loved the church and gave himself up for her. . . . Even so husbands should love their wives as their own bodies. He who loves his wife loves himself. For no man ever hates his own flesh, but nourishes and cherishes it as Christ does the church because we are all members of his body."

These are scarcely the words of a misogynist! Rather, they form a melody of sublime love, comparing human marriage with the divine one. Paul's sense of paternal authority, derived from Jewish tradition, forms the framework of the marital relationship, but within that framework is the dynamic of pure love and respect. Paul has complex views about women's status, but it is plain that contempt for women does not underlie any of his viewpoints. In Corinthians he even establishes an equality of conjugal rights: "But because of the temptation to immorality, each man should have his own wife, and each woman her own husband. The husband should give to his wife her conjugal rights, and likewise the wife to her husband. For the wife does not rule over her own body, but the husband does; likewise the husband does not rule over his own body, but the wife does. Do not refuse one another. . . ."

Thus, Paul recommends not only marriage, but also a companionable sexual equality in which women have access to their husbands on the same terms as husbands have access to them. One senses that Paul believes wholeheartedly in a companionable marriage and that marriage is good. He establishes husbands as heads of households, but the relation is to be tempered by love, companionship, and mutual delight. So deep is his concern for a proper, Christian sexuality within the confines of marriage before God that he urges partners never to refuse each other, that is, never to drive the partner into the arms of someone else.

However, Paul's deepest wish is that many Christians remain celibate because such persons serve God without diversion: without dividing loyalties between God and spouses and children. "It is well for a man not to touch a woman," he wrote, not because women are evil, but because of the "temptation to immorality." This is so, not because women are wicked or unclean or inferior—that sort of misogyny has cropped up in the church at times, but it is totally un-Christian—but because sex is so often misused and because sex can be a major stumbling block in a person's relationship with God. Over and over in his letters Paul alludes to the war between the carnal impulses and the spiritual life. Celibacy, then, is even better than marriage, though he hastens to say that there is no evil in marriage. There is simply less chance of a pure spirituality within it. His famous dictum that it is better to marry than to burn is not based on a hatred of sexuality, but rather on a distaste for immorality, as well as an appreciation that a "burning" single person cannot very well establish a good relationship with God. St. Peter's view of marriage closely parallels that of Paul. Both apostles prescribe a companionable union full of mutual respect and love, with males as the heads of the households. All the scriptural passages on marriage are gentle and emphasize reciprocal love; none could be classified as misogynist in any sense. There have been misogynists around the periphery of church history, but they are abhorrent to Christian values and should not be cited as evidence against the faith.

I believe that, from the biological and theological nature of things, there will always be in Christendom a tendency to make men the heads of households in a gentle and loving way. Nevertheless, in the best Christian marriages that authority will virtually disappear, melting into a complete companionable partnership in which the spouses achieve a spiritual, emotional, and physical unity that enables them to act in most instances with a single will. In any case, Christianity invites women to choose "the better portion" and to set aside as much drudgery as possible in order to concentrate on the education of the spirit and mind. I find nothing reprehensible in any of the Christian approach to marriage; indeed, except for Libbers, most women greatly relish a gentle male authority in their homes and over their children.

In the ranks of the Womens Liberation Army, however, Christian tradition is about as popular as a snake. The Lib line is that Christianity is sexist; the Jewish prophets and priests are indicted as sexist, along with the apostles, and the whole Judeo-Christian tradition was thus part of a dark episode in the history of "personkind" to cheat women of their birthrights. The Christians even defined God as Father and Son, which was a further humiliation for the female sex. In actual fact, He is without sex in any anthropomorphic form. As a movement, Women's Lib is strongly atheist or agnostic, as well as secular, although there are no doubt Christians in the ranks. Lib's most basic antagonisms are really directed toward the faith; its principal political alliances are with far leftist groups that are also sternly secular. Lib cannot possibly achieve its goals unless it first obliterates Christianity itself, along with the surviving ethic.

One reads the literature of Liberation with respect, if not awe. Amid the long lean prose one sniffs the gunpowder. The words march; the guerdons are flying, and the snare drums rattle their muffled beat. The Amazonian bugles have not yet sounded for the final battle, but one knows that, when they do, the target will be the Christian Church, with a few additional sallies against the Jews and Moslems. I hear the clank of armies rattling through the gloom of the 1970s, not only this woman's corps, but the battalions of the blacks, the companies of chicanos, the war parties of the Indians, and the echelons of the ethnics. I hear the scraping of trench shovels and the roar of treaded engines of war, all preparing for their assault on their oppressors, male Christian whites. They are readying their assault on me. By all accounts, I am oppressing multitudes of people, including those Junos whose army is girding for war. I expect some dark dawn to awaken surrounded, with Gloria Steinem and Ti Grace Atkinson commanding their legions out front, Carmichael and Cleaver on the flank, and perhaps Cesar Chavez at the rear, at which point I will pull the comforter over my head and commend my soul to God.

One reads Lib literature with the appreciation one gives to *Mein Kampf,* gingerly, but with an awareness that the blueprints are drawn and the orders of battle are issued. The casus belli is detailed on any newsstand, where one readily finds the works of Millett and Greer and Friedan, as well as a little paperback called *The New Feminism* by Miss Lucy Komisar. The book is a Lib manual for teenage girls: concise, readable, and fascinating for any male who perchance invades these precincts. Miss Komisar's prose marches. She appeals to her young converts with dignity and puissance. It does not matter, apparently, that the book is an intellectual disaster or that those poor teenagers will be given a wildly distorted estimate of the position of women in Christianity or in ancient or contemporary history.

Consider Miss Komisar's summation of St. Paul:

Saint Paul, considered one of the prime woman-haters of his day, said that man was not created for woman, but that woman was created for man. He also had a loathing of sex and said, "it is not good for a man to touch a woman." However he recommended that people get married if they could not overcome their sexual instincts ("It is better to marry than to burn.").

He also disliked women who spoke for themselves—especially when they disagreed with men. [?] "Let the women learn in silence with all subjection," he declared. "Wives, submit yourselves to your husbands."

Saint Paul's letter of instructions to the Corinthians established the place of woman—on the bottom. "The head of every man is Christ; and the head of the woman is the man," he told them.

This sort of thing might best be described as intellectual rape. It is the sort of scholarly ripping of which Mailer convicted her Liberationist sister, Millett. Several points are in order:

—The apostle who stands accused of hating women is the very one who advises husbands to love their wives as much as their own flesh.

—The apostle who stands accused of putting women under complete subjugation is the one who advises wives that they have access to their husbands' bodies on equal terms and that their husbands owe their wives utmost consideration.

—The apostle accused of loathing sex actually prescribed it in marriage and urged partners not to withhold it from each other. Indeed, he urged marriage upon those who could not contain themselves in single life.

—The apostle who is accused of hating and fearing women who "speak for themselves" or who disagree with men is the one who suggests that women discuss their concerns with their husbands and whose strictures had to do only with church propriety during worship.

—The apostle accused of loathing sexuality is the one who sees it as an impediment to a spiritual union with God. Paul does not loath sex; he subsumes it to the more important business of building human spirituality. It is not an either-or matter with him, but the establishment of priorities and values. One more quotation is in order:

The unmarried man is anxious about the affairs of the Lord, how to please the Lord; but the married man is anxious about worldly affairs, how to please his wife, and his interests are divided. And the unmarried woman or girl is anxious about the affairs of the Lord, how to be holy in body and spirit; but the married woman is anxious about worldly affairs, how to please her husband. I say this for your own benefit, not to lay any restraint upon you. . . .
(I Cor. 7:32)

St. Paul was greatly concerned about decorum in worship when he wrote the tumultuous Corinthian church, and his guidelines were not grounded in misogyny. Much of that portion of Corinthians, in fact, is devoted to fit conduct; he discusses, for instance, the impropriety of allowing too many people to prophesy or speak in strange tongues.

In her rush to condemn anything remotely Christian or Jewish, Miss Komisar produces some rather curious interpretations of the story of Adam and Eve in Genesis: "The men who wrote the Bible [note the planted axiom] condemned Eve. The book of Genesis in the Bible states: 'Unto the woman Eve he said, I will multiply greatly thy sorrow and thy conception; in sorrow shall thou bring forth children and thy desire shall be to thy husband, and he shall rule over thee.' "

She lets it go at that. Not a word about the even more severe curse on Adam. Moreover, she is content to attribute the curse on Eve to "the men who wrote the Bible," even though these writers penned an even more terrible curse upon their own sex. Of course, no Jewish prophet would have dared to quote Jehovah without an inner certitude that what he received was inspired by the Holy Spirit. Is Genesis, then, some sexist plot? Miss Komisar certainly wishes her teenage readers to think so, but one cannot help wondering why such "sexists" condemned Adam to scratch a living by the sweat of his brow from a soil that yields thistles and thorns. If it was a sexist plot, it surely boomeranged.

It begins to grow clear why question marks surround Lib's methods, scholarship, and goals. A movement that cannot ground itself in truth, carefully and objectively considered, is suspect in all it does and advocates. One thing is certain: Libbers love to dwell upon their persecutions almost as lasciviously as liberals love to scare themselves with the evil ghost of Joe McCarthy. One cannot, after all, have a going movement unless one can demonstrate that women have been trapped in the catacombs since the dawn of creation. To bend the future, it is necessary to twist the past.

III

No matter whether the story of Genesis is allegory or truth, the curse on both Adam and Eve has been operative through the millennia to the present day. From time immemorial, women have been subject to their husbands or guardians, and in the process they have lost some of their wealth and freedom.

That can scarcely be argued. Whether this came about as the result of male malice toward women or base greed or a conscious or unconscious conspiracy is another matter and one that Lib needs to examine further. It is one thing for men to be mistaken, quite another for men to engage in a deliberate conspiracy to deny so large a portion of humanity some basic protections and liberties.

Miss Komisar devotes several chapters of Lib gospel to the history of male chauvinism. Her targets turn out to be most men of any prominence, ranging from Hitler and Goebbels in modern times, together with Dr. Spock, to Aristotle and Plato, with stops at all the way stations in between. It is not difficult, when your target is as broad as the other half of the human race, to populate your rogues' gallery with some prize specimens of misogyny. The difficulty with that is that it is equally easy to fill a similar portrait gallery with men who have felt and expressed profound respect for women. The collection of a few dozen misogynist statements, ripped helter-skelter from a few dozen cultures and nationalities and epochs, proves nothing at all, just as a similar collection of opposing views and personalities from such diverse cultures and times would hardly be convincing. It is doubtful that, even within a single culture at a single time among men with similar social views, misogyny could be positively identified. A woman's virtue in one culture might be a liability in another. Women of good, strong, independent character, such as we celebrate in our pioneers, might be thoroughly condemned as barbarous creatures in some other social context. Moreover, at times the sexes have ambiguous feelings about each other. The same male who derides a woman's "muddleheadedness" may greatly admire her incisiveness, wit, or ability to deal with tradesmen. Conversely, the woman who admires aggressiveness in men may also resent their lack of sensitivity or tenderness. The opinions of each sex about the other are riddled with ambivalence. Moreover, opinions shift with growing maturity. The views of a man of 60 about women may be quite different from those he held in adolescence.

Thus, a simple roll call of rogues is inane. Each life of each rogue must be considered in its milieu and evolution. One searches for such a reasonable sophistication in Lib literature, but it is lacking. The tendency is to fire at anything in trousers and support anything in pantsuits or skirts. The effort seems to be directed at proving persecution, as if womankind could garner greater sympathy by demonstrating that the sex had lived in a spiritual Dachau since creation. I wonder why. What had Kate Millett to gain from savaging a few literary rogues? What had Miss Komisar to win from an apparently conscious effort to twist the love and spirit of St. Paul? Why not let the case rest simply on its merits? Is the case so weak that it is necessary to exaggerate it wantonly to be persuasive? Whatever the reason, the methods are unscrupulous, as I will set out in detail below.

Of course, a militant enterprise without its devils is like a religion without its god. Social movements necessarily paint dark pictures of bleak persecutions to inspire proper allegiance. That is why the liberals rehash the McCarthy era so lovingly: he is a genuine devil! Things are rarely as bad as such movements portray them, and that is why ideologies brazenly rewrite history to fit their propaganda. It must gall the sisters of liberation to discover myriads of women who *like* men, enjoy their current status, and refuse to support Lib. Perhaps these calculated distortions are designed to make converts, but ultimately reality intrudes, and they defeat the enterprise. That should cause no surprise. The wild tactics characteristic of so many ideologies seem to conceal a death wish. One wonders, for example, whether the radical Weatherman SDS faction hungers at some fathomless level to be caught and stopped. It is surely true that ideologies, unlike Christianity, embody within themselves the seeds of their own annihilation and that these seeds flourish in the soil of untruth. Miss Komisar refers casually to "several thousand years of misogyny" as if it were a demonstrated fact. Such things are the substance of the Goebbels big lie. There are grains of truth, areas of believability in such a casual indictment of the male sex, but I find myself flooded with skepticism. The sexes know each other too well. I know women too well, and women know me too well; there are bridges across the gulf, bridges of tenderness and love and simple companionableness. The bonds that unite lovers and husbands and wives are too numerous and strong. The big lie finds its haven, like all perversions, mainly among the psychopaths.

I suppose that a rigorous inquiry would reveal a broad spectrum of relationships between the sexes and that a few of these could spring from misogynist concepts. Nevertheless, the bulk of what has been denounced by Lib as misogyny in reality had its origin in chivalry, which has at its root the desire to pay homage to a pure and fair sex. One can agree that the chivalric ideal has in some respects limited the freedom and property of women, one can agree that women are not really so weak that they need chivalric protection, and yet not be forced to the conclusion that chivalry conceals some base contempt or covert hostility to womanhood. Unfortunately, Miss Komisar's teenage audience will not be afforded the opportunity to make careful distinctions or to separate mistaken ideals from male malice.

One hears much of the conspiracy theory of history. It forms the basis of the radical right's conception of modern events, for example, that capitalism is controlled by "Jewish financiers" or that Dwight Eisenhower was an unwitting or knowing agent of the Communists. The theory undergirds the liberal conception of the right wing; for example, liberals perceive of McCarthyism as a conspiracy and sincerely believe that most conservatives are conspiring to silence them. Protestants have frequently attributed conspiratorial motives to Catholics. Southern plantation owners regarded abolition as a conspiracy. There are in fact actual conspiracies, such as the Comintern or the coordinated bombings by the SDS in the 1960s. It is nonetheless astonishing to discover in Lib literature a tacit assumption that the male sex—half the human race—has knowingly conspired to suppress the deepest aspirations of the other half throughout history. Most of what is labeled conspiracy by ideologues is actually the simultaneous evolution of a viewpoint in diverse areas, which results in the harmonic activity of independent but like-minded people acting on their beliefs. Those who discover conspiracies where there are none are ipso facto trying to bend the past and present to fit their conception of the future. A mythical male conspiracy forms the foundation for a conscious new female conspiracy that seeks, not so much equality, but domination of Western society. Although Lib is not in itself a conspiracy, there are conspiratorial elements within its confines—one thinks of the militant Ti Grace Atkinson—whose object is something other than the heterosexual equality sought by most Libbers.

In any case, the male sex stands accused of the widest conspiracy in history, the suppression of women. Men may have been mistaken: men may have legislated protection for women barring them from some employment and denied them some civil liberties from an erroneous assumption that they were weaker. However, it is not error that Lib perceives in history, but something darker and more malevolent. In truth, there are relatively few males who ever concern themselves with a conscious domination of women, and these have been generally on the weak fringe of manhood. The run of men have never been concerned with which sex is superior or inferior, more or less intelligent, more or less aggressive, or more or less virtuous. It is one of the oddities of Lib thought that they assume that the question smolders unremittingly in the male mind. Neither do most men entertain a chronic fear of "threatening women" who excel in careers or moneymaking. The great majority of men do not harbor such fears because women are not frightening. Significantly, there is no organized Male Lib among men, even though a case could be made that one is needed, for instance, in divorce and alimony matters.

If Women's Lib is ever to acquire a mass base beyond the chic intelligentsia, it must address itself to reality and abandon the merely polemic role in which it is now ensnared. Many women have no attraction to Lib, even though they see things that cry out for remedies. It did not take Lib to tell them that even in the English-speaking nations, they have lacked economic opportunity and some social freedoms; George Bernard Shaw caught the English attitude perfectly in *Pygmalion*. But most women know things that Lib refuses to recognize: that the hope of happiness and opportunity rests not so much in changing the social milieu as in the merit, pluck, wisdom, good grace, and determination of each woman who wishes to improve her status. In that respect, self-fulfillment differs not a particle from the self-fulfillment of men. These women know, as well, that their husbands, sons, and lovers are not Bluebeards, not the monsters who people the dark forests of the feminists.

IV

To grow up as a girl is to grow up stultefied, passive, and servile, writes Miss Komisar bitterly. She dwells at length on the forces that mold boys and girls, and she concludes that girls are short-changed. Girls are wrapped in pretty starched dresses and must sit quietly playing with dolls, tea sets, and toy vacuum cleaners, while boys get dirty and roughhouse and have fun. Boys learn to be adventurous, active, and aggressive, while girls learn to paint and play with dollhouses. Boys learn competitive games such as baseball, while girls skip rope. Boys get trains and cars and chemistry sets and soldiers while girls get clothes. Boys fly kites, climb trees, explore caves, catch frogs, take old clocks apart, build models, and organize gangs, while girls wield toy mops. The list is endless.

Miss Komisar paints a melancholy portrait of suppressed personality, a rigorous sex-role training that begins virtually in infancy and ends up with the creation of adult female vegetables. Men get all the breaks. Miss Komisar's bitterness weaves its iron thread through the whole chapter. It is the *cri de coeur* of a woman who senses that her sex has betrayed her, that her parents, her teachers, her religion, her textbooks, her society, her government, and above all, men have stunted her growth and forged her chains. I do not doubt her sincerity, but I confess to having grave doubts as to her accuracy. I do not believe these pathetic descriptions of girlhood are true or real. There is something desperately warped about her, and Lib's, elaboration of girlhood and boyhood as it has existed in the United States. After reflecting some while on my own childhood, I concluded that her portrait of savagely repressed womanhood is grotesquely wrong and unreal, although a tiny minority of American girls may have experienced something of what she describes.

My own childhood was quite typical. I lived in a middle-class, midwestern suburban neighborhood, among people with diverse religious and ethnic backgrounds and in the midst of a great pack of girls and boys of assorted ages and sizes. The girls I knew were not at all confined to "organdy dresses" or any other kind of garment, although those who attended a parochial school wore blue uniforms. In fact, I scarcely saw them in dresses at all. They wore jeans and sneakers and blouses and sweaters, and for a very practical reason: they were full partners in our boisterous play. We played tackle football, sandlot baseball, hide and seek, badminton, and basketball. We roller-skated, swam, played hockey and badminton, wrestled, and once in a while rode horses, all with a grand disdain for sexual differences. We engaged in fierce thornapple fights, in which the girls were, if anything, more treacherous than the boys. During those World War II days we jointly built forts to fight the Nazis. One summer we built pushcarts: three girls constructed one, two boys and a girl the other. On the day of the big race the girls won because their cart was lighter and easier to push. It was those girls, too, who harnessed their German shepherd to a toboggan.

If they had dolls and tea sets, they shared such curiosities with the boys; and if the boys had erector sets and toy armies, they were duly shared with the girls. No activity was exclusive: coloring books, Parcheesi, Monopoly, checkers, assorted card games, circuses, and carnivals were all joint projects. There were moments when formal behavior was required, moments when it was necessary to be "a gentleman" or be "a lady," but these were only occasional. Most of the time we fished together, caught polliwogs together, set up tents together, skated and sledded together, and waited together for trains to flatten a penny put on the rails. I do not believe that things have changed, nor do I believe the childhood I have described to be untypical in the United States, although parental supervision has, unfortunately, made grave inroads since my childhood in the late 30s and 40s, as, for example, in the Little League.

Neither was there a sharp delineation of sex roles in the household chores we performed. All the youngsters had such tasks as doing dishes, making beds, emptying garbage, keeping their rooms clean, shoveling walks, emptying wastepaper, and mowing lawns. The girls, however, had more heavy housework, and the boys were generally assigned such yard work as weeding gardens and cutting lawns, but even these activities were by no means exclusive. Of course, in time, the sex roles did manifest themselves. In junior high the boys encountered shop

73

and mechanical drawing, while the girls faced domestic sciences. Even here, however, there were areas of mutual endeavor, such as typing classes or instrumental music.

Miss Komisar cites segregation of recesses and classrooms as part of the problem but, at least in my experience through grade school, no such segregation existed. Recesses were coeducational, no matter whether they were devoted to baseball, kickball, or Red Rover. Further, we were generally seated alphabetically in classes, without regard to sex. I beg the reader's forgiveness for delving into my childhood at such length, but the purpose is to demolish Miss Komisar's bizarre description of girlhood, a picture that demonstrates perfectly the disjunction between Lib ideology and reality. Her prim organdy version of girlhood is bunk, and her dark commentary on the mutilation of girls' personality is wild fantasy. She herself admits that girls win the bulk of scholastic honors, and that in itself suggests that girls are not repressed intellectually by their sex role. She has things all warped: most girls like being girls and would not willingly trade sexes. While cultural influences do mold their personalities toward an ideal called femininity, it can scarcely be argued that such stimuli are any more destructive than the influences that mold boys toward an ideal of masculinity. The evidence of damage just does not exist.

Miss Komisar proposes some changes in the school system that I consider valid. Girls should have access to technical and mechanical classes if they choose. They should be encouraged to consider the higher professions, including law and medicine, as well as architecture, business management, and engineering. If they choose a field such as engineering, they should be encouraged and should have access to all the mathematics and chemistry and physics they require. I do not believe that they are denied these things now: especially in new fields such as computer programming and data processing, access has been wide open. There may be a certain amount of social pressure that pushes each sex toward its orthodox role, but it is not tyrannic or insurmountable; it is a rare girl who is prohibited from entering any field she really wants to study.

V

A few years ago, when I was working on the editorial page of a daily paper in Montana, I cast a baleful eye on two young Lib ladies adorning our news staff and decided to do a column, just for fun, that would enrage the dears. So I duly recorded all the misogynist bromides I could remember about the female sex, gradually escalating the attack until I was sure the ladies would be simmering. At the end, however, I gave my game away, I supposed, by finishing off with a couple of absurd non sequiturs. I declared that no decent President had been elected since the advent of woman's suffrage and that we had since been in a state of continuous war. I assumed that would reduce all their indignation to merriment. And so the column went to press.

I misjudged. No sooner was the piece in print than the Woman's Artillery Corps began lobbing its howitzer shells into my office. For days the missiles rumbled in like buzzbombs gliding down on bomb-rocked London. Letters, calls, screaming denunciations, and personal visits. The bulk of them did not bother to assail my argument; they assailed *me*. I filled the letters column with these marvelous libels, which informed the world that obviously I feared castration; that I was clearly sick, sick, sick; that I was no doubt the victim of an inadequate sex life; and that I must be surrounded by horrible women. I was hanged in effigy by the ladies of the circulation and advertising departments. One thing I learned for certain: Women's Lib Is Nothing To Joke About. I emerged from Coventry some days later, sadder and wiser and persuaded that the female sex need never worry about being dominated by anything or anybody. In fact, I regard as slightly deranged anyone who argues that females are the more delicate sex. Whatever Miss Komisar's "thousand years of misogyny" has accomplished, it has not succeeded in intimidating the ladies.

All of this is a roundabout introduction to the idea that women are, if anything, tough. William Ross Wallace, who concluded that the hand that rocks the cradle is the hand that rules the world, was neither stupid nor obtuse. One of the great curiosities about Lib is that it arrived hard on the heels of a widespread literature about dominant females. Lib was aborning even while numerous intellects were seriously examining the emerging American superwoman and her impact on hapless males. There had been a decade or so of entertainments built around bumbling husbands and superwives who could fix anything with the twist of a hairpin. Beyond that, the nation had been drenched with the statistics of triumphant womanhood: not only did they own most of the wealth, but they did most of the family buying, right down to their husbands' skivvies. The power to buy for the whole family was the power to establish its way of life and even to define the husband's picture of himself. Put him in a sports shirt and cotton chino pants and he is likely to think of himself in a different light than if he were in blue jeans and a Western shirt! It was a time when sociologists were probing the deterioration of American manhood, along with the growth of surrogates such as football-watching. Men were defined as Ozzie Nelson types, reduced to wearing Burmuda shorts in backyards, where they were permitted to cook steaks, not too expertly, on the barbecue. It was a time when the Dagwoods had been defeated and the Blondies were triumphant. The physical softness and overweight of American men had so alarmed the Kennedy administration that it launched a fitness crusade and popularized jogging and leanness. It even idolized "toughness" in men and sought that quality within its ranks.

Lib had other notions, however. At the very time when, by all serious estimates, American men were being submerged in a matriarchal or at least female-oriented culture, Lib introduced anew the myth of the barefoot, pregnant, persecuted second sex. I have often wondered whether Lib is really a struggle against the intolerable persecution of women, as its ideology proclaims, or is actually a brilliant, albeit unconscious, effort to consolidate the triumph of women in technological mass society over men, in much the way Liberalism uses the McCarthy episode to maintain its dominant cultural position. It is true, nonetheless, that women had less career opportunity and lacked wage parity with men, despite their economic power as buyers in the market place. Part of that lack of opportunity was the fault of legislators who scarcely dreamed that women might wish to be plumbers, miners, or bombardiers. Lib has never been content to limit its bill of grievances to economic matters; the argument, rather, is that women have been systematically repressed in every facet of life: in law, marriage, employment, medical care, religion, and parenthood.

The Libbers were particularly incensed about sexual exploitation. And here they had a point, so long as they limited the particulars to Hugh Heffner and all the disciples of his libertine *Playboy* philosophy. Lib chose, instead, to indict the whole male sex, and there was even a spate of huffy letters in the papers about men who glance appreciatively at a woman's figure on the streets. In other words, Lib indicted us all.

A whole ideology of "male control" rests on the assumption that women are treated purely as sex objects and that men conspire to keep women in servitude, or domestic slavery, by forbidding them contraceptives, abortions, and freedom to "control their own bodies." All of which is surely one of the strangest arguments ever invented by the Amazons. *Playboy* types do treat women as sex objects; some men do exploit the sexuality of women. They are not, however, the same men as those who resist abortion or contraception, or both. Far from being hedonists, the latter are usually moralists and religious. Their intent is precisely to give women control over their bodies by encouraging chastity and by linking chastity with the very serious business of bringing new life into the world. It is precisely the playboys of the world who are most liberal about abortion. The ones who treat women as bodies, as sex objects, are the ones most eager to evade the consequences of sex. Lib ideology, however, attacks the male sex broadside as a conspiracy to reduce women to sexual slavery. This attack evades the most fundamental question about abortion: whether it takes the life of an emerging person who is wholly different from the mother. It is that question that produces anxiety about abortion in the men and women who question it. Lib ideology defines heterosexual relations as a cheat and a trap. There is no joy in courtship, no pleasure in pursuit or attractiveness, and no joy in the marital communion.

This ghetto ideology has attracted large numbers of women who find in its self-pitying parameters a measure of their own unhappiness. Lib ideology rationalizes housework, boredom, low-level jobs, distaste for conjugal relationships, and frustrations. It may be theater of the absurd, but it matters not so long as it provides a rationale for the discontents of being a woman. It flourishes as an ideology only through the promiscuous use of blinders. Lib only reluctantly confesses that women enjoy being mothers, and it is commonplace to accuse those who do of using motherhood to conceal their mediocrity. Neither does Lib concede a woman's pleasure in being protected by the arms of a strong man, a strong husband who can fend off the werewolves that circle many a home even in these civilized times.

A great many women are fully aware of what it is like to be male, and they want no part of the curse of Adam. They know about the assembly line automatons who pull the handle of a punch press all day or screw the same type of nut on the same type of bolt for eight hours each day of their lives to earn their bread. They know all too well the drudgery of bakers and shoe salesmen and accountants and TV repairmen and waiters. They know that very few glamorous and fascinating jobs exist in the world for either sex, and that most male work is dismally routine and frustrating in its sameness. Very few men can be brain surgeons or history professors or CIA agents. Perhaps 90 per cent of all labor, both men's and women's, is sheer drudgery, and even in the so-called glamour positions 90 percent of the job is routine. It is rather rare, for example, that a reporter gets his teeth into a good story: most of the time he deals with births and deaths and weather and paving contracts. There is little difference between pushing a broom and screwing in light bulbs as a school janitor and vacuuming the house as a wife; there is little distinction between pulling a punch press handle all day in a machine shop and preparing one more of an infinitude of dinners for a hungry family. In fact, a woman at home can at least arrange her day. If there is an exhibition at the art museum, she can arrange to see it; if there is a tea in the afternoon, she can arrange to attend. She is not tied down as relentlessly as those who suffer the curse on Adam. She has the opportunity to read, cultivate herself, do hospital work, have a social life; if she is bored, she can blame only herself. Most women are not convinced that the grass is that much greener on the other side, and that is why they look at Lib with amazement and skepticism.

Despite all the evidence to the contrary, Lib ideology goes to extreme lengths to describe women as basically weak and massively dominated by men. One of the striking paradoxes of Lib ideology is its insistence that women are so weak that they are heavily dominated by men, but so strong that the chivalric code is absurd. The feminists, insisting on women's weakness, even argue that men define women and impose upon them the values that govern their entire lives. Here is Miss Komisar on the topic:

The sex-role system robs a woman of her identity. In this society, women are defined by men. Their own status in the community is determined largely by their husbands' achievements, and even when they receive recognition in their own right, newspapers identify them as Mrs. John Jones. . . .

Men also define women's attitudes about themselves. A "feminine" woman is pleasing—and not threatening—to a man. A "good wife" supports her husband's ego. . . . [She fails to add that a good husband supports his wife's ego, and is pleasing, and not threatening to his wife!]

Men also define what is considered "womanly" or "feminine." These adjectives are applied to women who are pliant, compliant and anxious to please men. . . . A woman must practically efface herself. . . . [I have yet to find a man who actually wants a self-effacing limp dishrag for a wife. Of course, he wants a woman anxious to please him; he is equally anxious to please her!]

Ultimately, according to the male definition of "true womanhood," women exist for men—to please them and serve them. . . .

This is nonsense. Where do Libbers acquire the notion that men seek female slaves and feel threatened by successful women or that men want limp wives? The argument seems masochistic, and one senses just under the surface a wish that American men would be more dominant and paternal. I have not discovered in my life a single American male who has failed to applaud his wife's achievements and successes, from simple motherhood to professional skill. It makes his own life all the richer to have such an accomplished and engaging mate. There no doubt are some males who dread any evidence of evolution in their wives, but they are the weak fringe, with their own wobbly egos under pressure.

77

Apart from simple social custom, for example, "Mrs. John Jones," nearly all the defining of women is done by women. The only major exception is the church, in which a basically male ministry, relying on Scripture and other teachings, has authoritatively defined women's roles in family and religious, but not in economic, life. Much of the defining of women occurs in the women's media, where women editors and writers handle the women's pages of newspapers and produce women's magazines and help create women's daytime TV. Women define themselves, not only in the media, but in innumerable women's clubs, *pro bono* groups, and societies such as the League of Women Voters or the American Association of University Women. All of them form a dynamic, female-directed program of value-development for women. One can agree that some women are submerged in their husbands' and sons' successes and failures, but the fact that custom makes a woman Mrs. John Jones instead of Mary Maidenname is scarcely evidence that women are an oppressed class or male-directed robots.

My instinct tells me that each sex has its positions of superiority and inferiority, its advantages and disadvantages. Men may have more career opportunity, but women have more control over their daytime hours, hence the freedom to cultivate themselves more readily. Men may see more of the world, but women reap more of the joys of parenthood and the pleasures of family life. Men may engage more often in public affairs, but women need not surrender two years of their lives to military service or face death and maiming in war. I wonder how many Libbers have wandered the corridors of Veterans Hospitals and old soldiers' homes to see the maimed, the blinded, the basket cases, and the insane who willingly, often proudly, marched off to desperate war for the safety of their wives and sisters and mothers and for a nation and society in which men could be free. It is difficult to understand why Libbers feel so cheated and short-changed. The tragedy of such envy is that there is so little to envy.

VI

She walks in beauty, like the night
   Of cloudless climes and starry skies;
And all that's best of dark and bright
   Meet in the aspect of her eyes:
Thus mellowed to that tender light
   Which heaven to gaudy day denies.

One shade the more, one ray the less,
   Had half impaired the nameless grace
Which waves in every raven tress
   Or softly lightens o'er her face;
Where thoughts serenely sweet express
   How pure, how dear their dwelling place.

And on that cheek and o'er that brow
So soft, so calm, yet eloquent,
The smiles that win, the tints that glow,
But tell of days in goodness spent,
A mind at peace with all below,
A heart whose love is innocent!

Lord Byron's poem is undoubtedly pure sexism. Not only does it stress such ephemeral things as inner beauty and grace; it also seems to glorify brainlessness and innocence. Therefore Lord Byron is contemptible, and his sexism deserves prominent display in Lib's Rogues' Gallery of despicable males. Enough of "nameless grace"—the time has come for women to plunge into the man's world and become sophisticated, adventuresome, aggressive, and a threat to men!

Unfortunately for Lib, dreams always have a price: something to be lost as well as something to be gained. Some of those traits that both sexes have heretofore cherished in women, traits well described by Lord Byron, cannot possibly reside in the soul of a cussing, sweating, cynical career doll. One usually does not, for example, discover those traits celebrated by the poet in the characters of female newspaper reporters or advertising copywriters. For some, the loss is inconsequential, and the access to a career, and what remains of the man's world, is well worth the price. That price, however, is often more dear than they realize in the flush of youth and liberation. It includes a barren womb, and that means an extremely isolated and lonely old age, where there is no younger generation to love or rely on for help; no grandchildren to spoil or enjoy, with that special rapport between the very old and the very young. The price goes even deeper than that. The wisdom of the run of mankind, in all its ages, cannot be lightly discarded. That wisdom about the existing role that women fill is constantly verified in the inner peace and happiness of countless women. There is a palpable danger that a woman who casts aside the maternal tradition also courts an inner turmoil and perhaps ultimately the solace of whatever pharmaceutical crutches she can find. Whether a woman's spirit, emotions, body and soul can all fit comfortably into the new mold proposed by Lib is a consideration that ought to be weighed carefully.

One of the most profound deviations being advanced by the feminists has to do with children. They propose to rid themselves of children, who are considered nuisances and impediments to the important business of a career. One discovers in Lib literature a womb-hatred, the feeling that the capacity to bear children is a rotten trick of nature that imposes domestic slavery on women. Most Libbers hate children; they make this abundantly clear. The best they can manage is the hope that kids will be antiseptically cared for by someone else, or at least that husbands, lovers—anybody—will share the task of changing diapers, babysitting, and making meals. This leads Lib to the strangest of all its demands: the "right" to 24-hour Federal child-care centers (why Federal?). Miss Komisar grumbles that Federal monies for such liberating enterprises are limited to helping welfare mothers, to the exclusion of other mothers who wish to be emancipated from their children and to be free to go to work. According to

Komisar, "all parents have a right to government supported child care." This makes sense only if we believe that we have a right to freedom from fear, a right to a job, a right to welfare, and a right to anything else that strikes our fancy—but no duties at all. The rationale is that professionals will, in any case, do a better job than poor ignorant mothers can, to the benefit of the children. Miss Komisar argues that the youngsters in the Israeli kibbutzes are better adjusted than those in families, but a kibbutz is scarcely a government child-care center; rather, it has the nature of an extended family, with a lot of "aunts" to care for the young. The Libbers' blithe willingness to abandon their children to institutions is a bit shocking, even if they show some desire for good institutions. One would expect at least some doubts about foisting standardized government values and propaganda on the young, about the impact of "professional child-care centers" on America's diversity and heterogeneity. That, however, does not seem to bother the Libbers. All this is not to suggest that child-care centers are all undesirable. Private ones may be a godsend to single mothers and a blessing to the community. Placing a child in them is now a matter of private contract: a woman may choose one that fits her family's ethics. Many are run by churches or charities.

Not only does Lib want to put the children out of sight once they are born; it would like to abort them before they are born. The feminists insist that legal restraints on abortion are forms of "male control" over their bodies. The notion runs counter to the simplest and most valid reality: except for rape, no man can possibly control the body of a woman. She always has the option of chastity, unless Lib wishes to argue that women are so weak that all sex activity occurs against their will. Most women have the additional option of contraception. Chastity may be a prickly subject among liberated Libbers, but the reality of it makes "male control" absurd. Historically, chastity has played a profound role in woman's character, not only because of social pressures and a sense of Christian virtue, but because of potential pregnancy. Far from condemning chaste women, men have traditionally praised them in poetry, song, fiction, courtship, music, philosophy, and religion. It is rather astonishing to see Libbers simultaneously assailing the double standard, which actually supports chastity in women, while they denounce men for making women sexual slaves. Moreover, while they denounce sexual slavery, which they discover in every admiring glance, they are determined to overturn all moral restraints on their sexuality and are off in hot pursuit of sensuality. One's mind refuses to accept such contradictions. Apparently Lib wants to be free (1) from all moral restraint, (2) from all maternal prospects and responsibilities springing from sexuality, and (3) from all male courtship and pursuit, all of which leads to lesbianism.

Listen to Miss Komisar on the topic: "The chief reason that feminists demand the right to abortion is that they believe women must have control over their own bodies. No woman ought to be forced to become an unwilling breeding machine to satisfy the beliefs or prejudices others hold about religion or a woman's role. Feminists say they will not give their bodies up to the control of the state." One wonders. Maybe they resist giving their bodies up to state control, but they have no compunctions about turning over the bodies and minds of their offspring to state control in government-sponsored child-care centers.

Apparently Miss Komisar has arrived at the indefensible conclusion that all women born into Catholic, Orthodox Jewish, or conservative Protestant families are "unwilling breeding machines" because these groups oppose abortion and because some oppose contraception as well. The conclusion is dubious, to say the least.

Any serious argument that women suffer from "male control" must rest on the notion that they are periodically ravaged and are always unwilling sexual partners. It must be assumed that resistance to abortion is based on the lust to enslave women rather than a desire to protect the developing child. It assumes that women have no option of chastity and that men are so overbearing that they can compel women to abandon their sexual scruples. It assumes that women never oppose abortion on religious grounds, and it must also assume that the fetus is a blob without rights rather than an evolving person. That, in fact, is Komisar's view exactly: "Scientists say that it [the fetus] is merely a mass of cells—that life does not occur until the infant is born." Unfortunately, she fails to reveal which scientists said anything like that, presumably because she wishes to protect their reputations. I find myself forced to the conclusion that Lib's male-control argument is the tender labor of crackpots. There is a silver lining, however: the ladies may sink Hugh Heffner without a trace and even force Norman Mailer to hide in Argentina.

VII

Fortunately, there is love. Most women find nothing repulsive about the comforts of a strong man's arms. If she provides a haven for him away from the tumults of the world, it is also true that he offers her a haven, a nest secure in love and freedom. Each sex helps mitigate the ordeals of the other; each supplies balm and understanding when the other's needs are profound. Love obliterates the tensions between the sexes and inspires each partner to seek the joy of the other. One does not discover, in the literature of Lib, much emphasis on love between the sexes, which is why the feminist movement seems so harsh, uptight, and naked. There is a great emphasis on self-esteem, or self-love, which can be a foundation for the love of others if it is employed properly and not allowed to remain a mere narcissism. There is some emphasis on sororal love, but very little on heterosexual love. There are concessions, of course, a softening of the harsh tones for men who understand Lib. For the most part, however, men are simply enemies, creatures to be defeated, persecutors. The feminists can hardly be lonely, for they lend each other generous emotional support in their battles with the Great Male Octopus. Still, the outreach of their love extends neither to children nor men: it embraces only themselves and the sisterhood, which is a multiplication of themselves. Such a narrow sort of love seems an insecure basis for joy in the world or for beatitude.

If, by putting a halt to some of the teenage euphoria that passes for love, they force men and women to reach across to each other in more rewarding ways, then perhaps their prickly ideology will lead to something valid. This, however, seems very improbable. Much more likely is the prospect that Lib will polarize the sexes. The result of Lib will not be unisex, but rather men and women so far apart, so distrustful and hateful, so antagonistic and competitive, so self-pitying that it will be almost impossible to bridge the chasm. That seems to be what is happening as Lib takes hold of the hearts of women. More and more conferences are for "women only" because men allegedly "wouldn't understand." Women are creating their own gynecological services because they refuse to trust male doctors. There is a growing Lib literature questioning the joy of heterosexuality. The feminists have gleefully discovered the female spider that stings its mate to death after mating, and their glee is not lost upon men. There is a tendency to treat men, not as individuals or persons, but as mere representatives of a dominant class, as an abstraction without character, ideals, passions, or beliefs. Because they loathe Man, the Libbers have lost contact with men. On the other side, men have begun joking, half in earnest, about the need for male liberation, as a means of protection. Consequently men, too, are beginning to think of Woman, instead of women. The Lib antagonisms are naturally provoking their counterparts in males.

While it is true that Lib has made men more aware of women's problems, knowledge is not empathy and understanding is not reconciliation, especially when Lib sees the world through such a distorting prism. If Lib ultimately prevents us from reaching across to the dear persons on the other side, then Lib will destroy something that most men cherish beyond price. Love between men and women is the great consolation in life, and it is what makes much suffering and many ordeals bearable. The Divine plan regarding sex roles was clearly ordained to prevent just such polarization and alienation between the sexes. A gentle male authority in family life was aimed at preventing just such a tragic competition and distrust from arising. The authority was created, not because one sex is superior to the other, but because it facilitates love that flows across the gap between two very different types of human beings. A Christian family becomes a unity because each of its members has a different and honorable role to fulfill and because it has a hierarchic structure rather than a chaotic egalitarianism. The mystery of marriage is that two become one; a man who damages his spouse or prevents her utmost fulfillment damages himself.

The most scandalous lacuna in Lib ideology is its failure to validate a middle ground. It insists on the sharp-horned dilemma of household drudgery or glorious career, with virtually no way stations between. The dilemma is unreal. There is nothing in the Judeo-Christian marital tradition that imposes such stark options on women. That can be seen readily enough through brief portraits of two real women who have built happy lives that combine the best of all worlds.

One is a school district psychologist who specializes in locating youths with learning disabilities and emotional problems. Her work is particularly rewarding, and she finds deep satisfaction untangling young lives and seeing the youngsters improve. She has a lawyer husband and five children. There is a housekeeper on hand for the younger ones when they come home after school. The psychologist has ample time for her family; she reads extensively, makes wines, takes her family on canoe trips, and is a good photographer.

Another woman I know is in her forties, has four children ranging from college age to junior high, and an executive husband. Each receives abundant love and attention. She has a paid position as the director of Christian education in her church; she is a national officer of her church, as well. She is active in the American Association of University Women and numerous other groups and clubs. She is an artist, skilled in a dozen crafts ranging from finishing driftwood to oil painting. She is an expert interior decorator, and has remodeled an old farmhouse, doing the rough work as well as the finishing. She is a skilled bargain hunter and antique collector. She reads a great deal and keeps up with politics and ideas. She plays the piano, entertains frequently, and finds time for innumerable charities and little thoughtful gifts.

Each of these women has thrust herself through the middle; neither is impaled on the horns of the Lib dilemma. They do not perceive of family life as an endless round of dishes, runny noses, and drudgery; in one of the families work is completely divided up between the youngsters, who have become capable cooks, housecleaners, and dishwashers. Each has an admiring husband who encourages his wife in every way. Neither would dream of throwing away the best of all worlds for the phantasmagorias of Lib.

VIII

We come to conclusions. Plainly, Lib is not ridiculous in so far as it can call attention to serious grievances in the field of employment. Nor is it noble: the self-pity running through its literature is disgusting. One finds warped perspectives mingled with valid hopes. Truth is treated cavalierly, and the movement's scholarship is shoddy and sometimes reckless.

A theoretical equality of the sexes is impossible to attain because of the innate differences between them. If it is nonetheless attempted in legal, educational, and vocational spheres, the result will be to cheat both sexes of their special prerogatives and greatly to reduce the mobility of all. Women need such things as dower rights, freedom from military service, and maternity leave. Men need job opportunity and can usually put an education to better use. The goal ought to be, not an abstract equality that refuses to recognize differences, but an open-door policy based on each individual case; there are women who would make brilliant engineers, and they should have the opportunity.

Each person has his own mountain to climb regardless of where he begins his life. In the end, his happiness rests not on a consciousness of the status of his class or genre, such as his sex, but on his merits and his willingness to work, to study, to adventure, to make friends, and to entertain novel ideas. Class status has little to do with a fruitful life; individual effort is infinitely more important.

As a Christian, I am reluctant to overturn the good tradition of the past or to defy what I believe is a divinely ordained hierarchy of family and church life. It does not matter to me one whit that the Boogeyboogey tribe in Willywacky have a matriarchy and a communal child-rearing system or that husbands there take their wives' family names. As a man of the West and the recipient of grace, I have inherited values that have produced a profound and spiritual love, an ecstasy, between the sexes, and which have contributed to peace, joy, amazing liberty, and a secure cocoon of stable family life for most children. The existing system is based mainly on nature and gives due weight to biological differences. The establishment of the Lib ethic can be accomplished only by defying nature as, for example, with abortion.

There is a need for some reforms. A just society should provide, for example, pay levels that are comparable for equal work. Even here, however, there are problems: employers often grant raises to men in *anticipation* that they will stay on and skip over raises for women in *anticipation* that they will not remain. Biology continues to obtrude. Much legal underbrush, such as laws enabling women to marry at an earlier age than men, could be cleared away.

The feminists are marching in an epoch when it is the vogue to organize all hopes, dreams, and hungers into a collectivist political enterprise. Thus, Lib is not unique. It is just one more among a dozen or two militant movements all clamoring for changes in law, all seeking a collective solution for problems that may be highly personal. Some day the phenomenon of militant movements will be seen as the hallmark of our times. Historians will look with great curiosity and pity at an age in which human beings could not conceive of any way to advance unless through lockstep political militancy and class warfare. In a sense, Lib is just another of the ideologies spawned from a Marxist class war dialectic. It is a perception of life based on the notion of an organized oppressor class, such as the bourgeoisie, or in this case, men, and an organizing oppressed class, such as women or the proletariat. The whole concept is really pathetic because it so violently and ruthlessly denies the human soul, God, and personality. One hopes that women will eventually rediscover the characteristics that distinguish their sex.

It is ironic that militant movements, ideologies, and politics only slightly change the nature of our civilization. They are deadlocked one against the other. The political uproars, the great lemming movements come and go, while the real revolution, the one that turns society inside out, is occurring in corporate boardrooms, on the drawing boards of engineers, and in the laboratories—that is to say, in those humble business precincts so despised by the militants. Our civilization will be transformed more by the lowly birth control pill than by Karl Marx and all his followers; more by the Wankel engine than by women's lib; more by Dr. Salk's vaccine than by the entire New Left. While the ideologists wrangle, the globe is being revolutionized by cost accountants and technicians and given meaning by religion. The future belongs, not to the demagogues and their cabals, but to scientists and theologians.

4

The Tentative
Citizen

I

Most Americans are provisional revolutionaries. There are few among us who have not entertained the thought that some day we might feel compelled to fade into the hills and mountains and from there wage relentless war upon the regime in Washington. For most of us the fantasy stops there, but in some, such as the Minutemen of the 1960s or the Weatherman faction of Students for a Democratic Society, the fantasy burst into reality in the form of paramilitary training or physical assault on people and property.

I once knew an editor of a large southwestern newspaper who argued seriously that it would be a fatal mistake for the National Guard to be Federalized. So long as the guard—the modern version of the state militias—remained under the command of the several state governors, there would be a subtle but profound check on the expansionist tendencies of the Federal government. That editor, too, was a provisional revolutionary.

The currents of hostility run deepest out on the fringes, although there are innumerable men of the center who could let themselves be goaded into armed resistance against the government of the United States. While some prefer exile, it must be remembered that exiles are abortive revolutionaries who find the regime unbearable and plan to wait for better days. A few Americans abroad even now will not return until Richard Nixon is no longer President. Had Senator George McGovern been elected in 1972, we might have seen the first great emigration from the United States. I know a family that planned to move to Australia or New Zealand—indeed, they still may if things, in their estimation, continue to deteriorate. Thus, in their own way they also nurture a provisional acceptance of the government in Washington.

A semirevolutionary stance is even more firmly embedded on the left than on the right. It begins modestly enough in routine liberalism with its resistance to

85

loyalty oaths, its cynicism about patriotic feelings, and its ultracritical attitude toward anyone in office who is not a simon-pure leftist. The attitude extends leftward with mounting intensity, beyond the avenues of social reform, out to the precincts of Ché Guevera and Mao Tse-tung, out to rural guerrilla action, underground life, and assassination. It is not far from the soirées of the chic Park Avenue radicals to the Black Panthers and ultimately to armed resistance against the government and active support of all its adversaries.

However, it is not only the highly ideologized who are provisionally loyal to the republic. In recent years businessmen of no particular ideology have exploded darkly and bitterly, mostly in private, against ominous new invasions of their entrepreneurial freedom. These muffled outcries can be dated specifically from the passage of the Occupational Safety and Health Act (OSHA) and similar laws in the last few years. The regulations promulgated to enforce OSHA are so complex that they fill pages of *The Federal Register* and reduce many businessmen to chronic criminals because it is impossible to comply with or even to be aware of all the obscure provisions of the act. Moreover, the act inverts the whole Anglo-Saxon concept of justice; inspectors are one-man prosecutors, judges and juries, and can impose warnings and fines at will. While the penalties can be appealed in court, it is cheaper for the entrepreneur to pay and confess "guilt" than to try to prove innocence.

I have sat astonished with a group of contractors who discussed the OSHA with such despair and choked emotion and resentment that their loyalty to the government was gravely weakened. This is not the place to discuss that law, but rather to point out that it and others like it are finally eroding the loyalties of middle America; the Kiwanis and Optimist and Lions Club members are bitter and frightened by the mounting volume of regulation and paperwork that besieges their small businesses. Whether the act was so grievous in itself or whether it was symbolic of the growing bureaucratic assumption that all businessmen are criminals, its net effect was to awaken hostilities and revolutionary fantasies among the most loyal and stable and fruitful citizens of the republic. That the situation is not worse can be ascribed only to the moderation of the Nixon administration in enforcing it and other laws, including the new consumer legislation. It is not that these businessmen oppose health or safety for employees or seek to cheat consumers, but rather that the law is drawn in a way that reduces them to second-class citizens in constant jeopardy.

The United States, despite its profound stability, has a long history of revolt. One needs only to recall some of the writings of Thomas Paine, or the Whiskey Rebellion, the Haymarket riot, the Hoovervilles, or the modern civil rights conflagrations to understand that, on the periphery of our political process, insurrection has always been regarded as a viable alternative. Even the Daughters of the American Revolution ultimately celebrate the overthrow of tyranny through a process of treason and revolt. The sort of tea parties that Boston has nowadays may not resemble the earlier and more famous gathering except in the fact that the chic radicals of that hub of learning feel the same way about King Richard as their forebears felt about King George.

Even though the revolutionary spirit has been part of the American tradition, it has never been dominant, except briefly during the Confederacy, when rebels achieved a political, but not cultural, disjunction with the Washington government and its adherents. Not until the 1960s did this red thread in our social fabric suddenly expand into the main design. It was not merely the ideologized at both ends of the political spectrum who harbored and nourished the dream of revolution; it was also the corner grocer and the tax accountant down the street and the current president of the local Optimists, who found themselves loathing and dreading a government that had declared them to be the real criminal class.

It is not that the bulk of Americans harbor the sort of Amerika-hatred that is common among the impatient young radicals. Neither is it that Americans everywhere are now marching to the fifes and snaredrums of modern Thomas Paines. Rather, it is that the disaffection became almost universal for the first time in our history, and some of that discontent spilled into the streets. Not even a saint in the White House could now allay the foreboding or restore the loyalties that were once the hallmark of the American republic. The Federal government is on probation. That raises questions that have been idle for a century: what is a valid state and to what extent are we obliged to heed its authority and obey its laws?

II

It is virtually impossible to define legitimacy in government. We can describe the salient aspects of a legitimate regime readily enough, but still have trouble separating legitimate governments from others. A legitimate regime must have continuity, permanence, authority, a constitutional basis in society, moderation, benevolence, and a nice regard for private freedoms, justice, and the consent of the governed. In addition, legitimacy is often tied to the peacefulness of the regime or its economic system. Sometimes a regime born in revolution, such as Red China, is considered illegitimate. If revolution is the key, then not only is the United States illegitimately governed, but so are France and the whole of Latin America.

In earlier epochs, when the West was perceived as Christendom, the problem was simpler. A legitimate regime was one that fostered Christianity, opposed heresy and paganism, and ruled by divine right. Kings and rulers were legitimate if they submitted to the faith and based their reigns on Christian values, particularly love, mercy, and justice. In our secular times the idea of legitimacy has grown out of that narrow Christian definition, but the roots of our present thinking still lead back to the earlier Christian concepts. Even the Theists who assembled our early national charters paid due homage to God, or Providence, as the ultimate source of the legitimacy of their new republican government in the New World. Thus, although the new nation was born from armed revolution, it was sanctified at once by recognition that Divine authority reigned over it and the American people. Only in recent years has there been any effort to divorce the government altogether from religious authority. At first it was done in the name of avoiding the transcendence of any sect or denomination, but now the effort is more candidly secular, agnostic, and atheist. If Christian values are still the source of legitimacy, then one could argue that the Franco regime in Spain, despite its extraconstitutional nature, is more legitimate than the United States government because it is more firmly Christian. Indeed, with the United States moving toward the abolition of all religious observance in its functions, any claim to legitimacy based on the old religious concept is nullified.

Despite its occasional aberrations, our government is benevolent and mild. Few would seriously argue otherwise, although there are many who believe that, if current centralizing and bureaucratic trends continue much longer, that benevolence will evaporate. It is also true that, while the government still functions with the consent of the governed, the grumbling and tentative rejection have increased. Its justice is essentially valid; its mercy is renowned; its continuity and stability are established; and its methods of transferring power have long since been validated. Thus, by most liberal and secular standards the government is legitimate, although the older Christian standards no longer seem to apply. At least from the Christian standpoint it can be argued that the regime is essentially neutral; it permits the faith to flourish as it will and does not tax establishments of religion or otherwise intervene in the practice of religion. Despite the Vietnam war and all the doubts it raised, it is folly to insist that the government is imperialist or warlike or militarist. We have been and are a nation of traders.

Thus, on virtually all secular and even some religious grounds, the government is legitimate. No one argues that a legitimate government is a blameless one; if that were true, no government would qualify. Rather, the question rests on the overall intent of the regime, and from that standpoint the government rests on ancient and honorable foundations. If the government is thus legitimately grounded, it has the right to formulate law and demand complete obedience to that law even if the law seems unwise or unjust to some. The magisterium of a regime cannot be lightly cast aside without unleashing all the unholy tendencies of man to plunder. Legitimacy validates treason and rebellion. That is to say, a legitimate and established regime has every right to regard treason against itself as a high and capital crime against the whole society and to regard insurrections as war upon the whole society. The less legitimate a regime—that is, in this instance, the less it rests upon the consent of the governed—the less valid is its suppression of rebellion and disloyalty. If liberals now disdain any public or private manifestation of loyalty to the country and ridicule the ideal of loyalty, perhaps they are revealing their belief that the United States government has lost is legitimacy and abdicated its claim to the allegiance of the American people.

Certainly, simple patriotism has ebbed to an all-time low. So far, only a few have crossed the Rubicon into the realms of rebellion, but their numbers expand daily and now include many thousands of draft dodgers and deserters living abroad. While a disaffected element always exists in any society, what is new in the United States is the middle American switch from wholehearted loyalty to tentative citizenship. What has departed is the unquestioning obedience to law and magisterial authority that was the hallmark of the nation. Its disappearance among middle-class citizens has been shocking, and our governors are even now unaware of the disaffection of middle America—an alienation that could result in new waves of disobedience, new troubles for enforcement agencies, and the drift of the less stable into militant hostility. Liberal leaders still encourage such defiance of order, describe the resisters as martyrs in good causes, and place the ultimate blame on the venality of the state. The liberals will be profoundly shocked in future years to discover that the resisters are not long-haired hippies promoting free sex and pot, but the Rotarian down the street who owns the hardware store. We will then see the beginning of a new liberal double standard: civil disobedience by young intellectual radicals will be expected and condoned, as always, but civil disobedience by the local undertaker or insurance salesman will be a manifestation shocking beyond words and something to be firmly dealt with by the police.

Beginning in the mid-1950s with the Negro revolution in the South and expanding in scope through the 1960s, the militance of the liberal clergy, both Catholic and Protestant, has fostered defiance of local, state and Federal law. Liberal Christian clergymen have, in other words, thrown the mantle of God and the holiness of Christ around the tumults. They have expressly sanctioned, not only the goal of uplifting the oppressed and miserable, of which most people approve, but also the method of civil disobedience to achieve these desirable ends.

As a general rule, liberal Christians have abandoned the older theology of reconciling unruly man with the will and purpose of God. The more modern theology begins with the proposition that God is a handy genie Who helps individuals free themselves to become whole and fulfilled persons able to use all their talents and resources to advance to comfortable economic levels and a measure of recognition in the community. Theirs is a man-centered religion: the church exists as a social agency; the clergy function as psychiatrists, counselors, and perhaps county extension agents. Thus, the liberal church becomes the enemy of the state wherever it discerns the state oppressing its subjects. There is abundant Christian teaching and scriptural authority for the belief that we should help others, give alms, love our neighbors and enemies, and comfort the distressed. The liberal theologians draw heavily on these injunctions and beliefs, but they depart from the more orthodox Christians by validating civil disobedience as the means to achieve these ends. More traditional Christians believe that the state is to be obeyed; that there are goals beyond this world and beyond our current appetites; and that fulfillment is ultimately perfect love between God and man. In short, those liberal clergymen who simultaneously preach civil disobedience and a doctrine of socialism in which the state succors the unfortunate by redistributing taxes they departed from established Christian doctrine. No matter how the brothers Berrigan justify their civil disobedience as a Christian gesture toward peace, they still have abandoned the teachings of the church when it comes to method.

The Christian position on civil disobedience, which has been expounded at length by both Peter and Paul, is worth examination. Even though we live in a secular age when the views of those two great apostles carry little weight among the run of men, their ideas can throw great light on what is happening in the

United States and what the result will be if civil disobedience becomes the rule in public affairs. There are implications in civil disobedience that radiate outward into family life, where the commandment to honor one's father and mother is affected, and into social and business life as well.

It is altogether possible that a chronically disobedient and rebellious people will push the government, by degrees, into an active and malicious tyranny when it learns to trust less and less the good will of the people. That regimes will persist in ruling and maintaining order there can be no doubt. That will happen by cruel means if necessary. Thus, the ancient Christian teachings on the duties of a citizen to his government and the duties of rulers to their subjects take on fresh relevance even in these secular times. It is possible that we may acquire a richer liberty only by heeding the teachings of the church.

III

The Bible is surprisingly silent about the relationship of Jesus to the government of Judea. One thing is certain: it offers no clear support to any secular faction that seeks to appropriate the words or behavior of Jesus on behalf of a political enterprise. The gospels are ambiguous and can be understood only in terms of the theocracy by which Judea was ruled. It is necessary to proceed with profound caution into the whole question because there are so many pitfalls and because so many secular factions clamor to claim Divine sanction.

The gospels record very little that Jesus said about the proper relationship of a man to his government. Later, St. Paul dilated extensively on the topic, as did other apostles, but Jesus was virtually silent. If the Jews were seeking a great leader who would free them from the boot of imperial Rome, Jesus sorely disappointed them. When questioned about paying taxes to the gentile Romans—a sore point with the Jews—Jesus merely urged them to render unto Caesar what was Caesar's and unto God what was God's. Thus, He really said nothing about the secular order imposed by Rome.

On the other hand, Jesus quickly organized a following and began preaching doctrines that were profoundly disturbing to the ruler-priests. Thus, He created a faction and engendered intense religious politics that grew so fierce that they led to the event of the cross. He organized His disciples and sent them out to the villages of Judea, preaching a doctrine of repentence. He sent them off unarmed, unfinanced, and with only the clothes on their backs, and He warned them that they would be persecuted and dragged before kings and rulers to give testimony to the new kingdom of heaven. Further, He admonished them not to fear those who could kill their bodies, but to fear Him who could cast their souls into hell—that is, to put the demands of God ahead of the requirements of temporal rulers. It is this statement that comes closest to undergirding the Rev. Martin Luther King's doctrine of civil disobedience, in which he asserts that one need not obey any secular law if it violates one's conscience. However, the King formula goes much farther than scripture does.

Jesus clearly knew that this new gospel He preached would generate controversy, that is, produce an intense politics in theocratic Judea, and He warned that He came as a divider; there would be ruptures henceforth, even within fami-

90

lies, over his doctrine. Controversy is the essence of politics, and thus Jesus was swept into the maelstrom of factionalism and opinion in His time. But if Jesus generated a fierce politics, it was surely the strangest politics the world had seen. It has no secular or temporal goal. There is not a scintilla of evidence that it sought to overthrow the existing rulers of Judea; indeed, Jesus absolutely rejected all efforts to make him king. Neither is there a shred of evidence that Jesus and his followers sought to reform the structure of the state. There is not a single word suggesting that the structure be altered, not a word implying that the state initiate social reforms, or egalitarian measures, or democratization of leadership, or a new relationship to Rome, or the elevation of a new priesthood, or the disbanding of the old elite. It is this total absence of any secular political or social goal in the enterprise of Jesus Christ and His disciples that shatters the claims of so many modern social gospel movements to the inheritance of Christianity. On the contrary, the doctrines that He taught were much more difficult and shocking; it was His intent not to overthrow rulers, but to call them to repentence, to bring them closer to the will of God, to replace sacrifice with mercy, and to replace the legalisms of the Mosaic law with love. Above all, the enterprise was to prepare the hearts of all Jews, the rulers and ruled, to accept the Messiah and his new covenant with all mankind.

Thus, there was launched a great enterprise—highly political and controversial—that nonetheless embodied no secular goal or reform. It could not be compared with the secular politics by which we choose and remove governors or the liberal politics by which we attempt to reform the social order and adjust the functions of government. Jesus proposed no social security or welfare systems, but He did command mercy and love and concern for the poor. He proposed no liberation from Rome, no Jewish sovereignty or buffer states or spheres of influence, and no ending of Judea's cold war with the Samaritans, but He did urge each of his followers to love his neighbor as himself, to love his enemy, and to do good to all.

The whole weight of the Bible indicates that Jesus treated the state as though it scarcely existed. He sought no ruling power and proposed no institutional reforms. A modern social gospel enterprise can claim to share His mercy and compassion, but not His method. At that point a great chasm looms between them, an unbridgeable gap between the kingdom of heaven built on the faith and behavior of individuals and the new Jerusalem built upon political and social power embedded in worldly law.

The gospel offers equally cold comfort to those defenders of the status quo who fail to see the misery and desperation around them or to those who believe merely in the survival of the fittest. Jesus was, indeed, a radical element in Judea, so radical that the conservative rulers sought to kill him. He mocked their authority, freely healing on the Sabbath. He addressed the elite harshly, calling them hypocrites and whited sepulchres, unclean inside, whitewashed outside. He rebuked their greed, their love of high status, and their propensity to burden widows and poor people with their legalisms. He assailed their lack of mercy and their obsession with ritual that meant little to God. In short, He shamed and publicly rebuked the elite of Judea and urged them to repent the arrogance that had led them so far from God.

Jesus did not abuse the rulers or insult them or shout uncivil epithets at them; there was always dignity and civility in his rebukes. He used no demagogic techniques. He aroused no mob. None of his methods could be used to justify the sort of rude, uncivil, obscene assaults on public tranquility that are commonplace to the New Left and the young radicals. Thus, it is difficult for any modern social enterprise—radical, liberal, or conservative—to lay claim to the authority of the Christian tradition. The man who pours chicken blood on draft records or marches with militant placards denouncing some aspect of society has no more claim on that moral authority than the cold, rich arrogant proponent of social Darwinism and the ideology of letting the devil take the hindmost. The city of God is not built with such stones. It is surely necessary to extricate the Christian faith from the embrace of every passing ideologue in and out of the church.

IV

The Rev. Martin Luther King proposed an attitude toward government that became the watchword of the 1960s in many circles. Dr. King, faced with Southern segregation laws, which he loathed and which had a cruel impact on his people, suggested simply that a law that was unconscionable need not be obeyed. Thus he set the stage for the endless confrontations and disruptions of the decade, as well as the malaise that still mantles the republic. His formula lent an air of legitimacy and sanctity to civil disobedience.

Dr. King was not blind to the necessities of the state; that is to say, he anticipated that defiance of the law could lead to enforcement of that law and to arrest and conviction of those who broke it. It goes without saying that this intelligent black leader was equally aware that his formula assailed the magisterium of lawful government. The very essence of law is that it falls equally on all, whether they agree or disagree with it. Rooted deep in Anglo-Saxon jurisprudence was the idea that just law must weigh equally on each citizen.

To all this Dr. King had a reasonable answer: the laws of the South isolated and degraded his people in a way that forbade even-handed justice. Moreover, the laws were enforced selectively: mildly for whites, harshly for blacks. It strained his conscience to acquiesce in laws that brutalized his people. Therefore, he would dramatize their evil nature as well as their unequal enforcement by leading a movement to defy them altogether. If there was any theological justification in all this, it rested on the Golden Rule and on the great commandment to love our neighbors as ourselves. There was also some support in the admonition of Jesus to fear God, Who had the power to cast the soul into hell, rather than fear rulers who had only the power to slay the body. All this came close, but only that far, to supplying a Christian rationale for the King formula.

The problem deepens when we consider the nature of conscience. The term is usually understood as that divinely inspired censor or policeman in the soul that alerts us to the wrong we do. Thus, our conscience is our inner policeman and law book, the source of our guilt and remorse and even our joy. If we let it, it governs our behavior. The question is, does an unjust law that we may resent actually invoke our conscience? One may surely loathe it and see its malevolent effect on others and yet, if there is nothing in the law that compels us to sin, does it offend our conscience? One may feel its bitter impact; it may tempt one to anger and resentment, but if nothing in the law compels us to sin or offend God, then conscience is scarcely applicable to the situation. It is not our conscience that is offended by segregation law, but our sense of justice and mercy. In fact, such laws were deeply unjust and hurt people, but if they compelled anyone to sin, it was the white man who believed in them out of his own false pride. The blacks were victims of unconscionable law, not perpetrators of it. A black man's response to such a law is to be aggrieved by its injustice to him, but not to feel that it offends his conscience. The guilty conscience belonged, and belongs, to the whites.

It is always best to separate our sense of injustice from our conscience. There may be innumerable unjust laws that we should seek to reform, but they are not a matter affecting our conscience or our relationship to God's will. The Christian formula is narrower. The implication in the teaching of Jesus was that a ruler could be disobeyed only when the ruler was demanding something that offends God; the emperor worship that Rome demanded from early Christians is an example.

Perhaps what Dr. King really meant to say was that unjust laws should be resisted because they encourage others to violate *their* consciences. If that is true, those who have the best case for resisting segregation laws are not the black victims, but those hardhearted whites who find in the law an opportunity to sin. It was the whites whose consciences were nagging them, but, of course they did nothing about these promptings. The principal reason for that is that the whites did not permit themselves to feel the sting of conscience or in some cases even admit that their consciences were bothering them. Consciences, we discover, are differing things. Each man's varies according to his upbringing, his religious training, and especially his openness to God. There are still relatively few Southerners who, in the quiet of their souls, will discover their own evil against their black neighbors.

Thus, Dr. King's formula is immediately confronted with a series of confusions. First, each conscience varies from the next and each man would thus become his own interpreter of law, obeying one and ignoring or defying another. Second, the formula confuses injustice with conscience. Third, it defies the idea that there is a public good: under his formula each man becomes his own emperor, doing as he pleases regardless of the settled opinions of the community. So what Dr. King was really discussing was law so unjust that disobedience was the only recourse of desperate men. There is a good argument for defiance if that sort of tyranny exists, as it sometimes does in the South. Such resistance has nothing to do with conscience, however, and in fact may deepen schisms and widen hatreds rather than heal the injustices.

In the case of unjust law, the proper recourse is reform, that is, public agitation and pressure and education designed to remedy the evil. As Dr. King well understood, however, there are circumstances in which reform is unavailing. In ancient Rome the early Christians were required to worship the emperor and observe other pagan customs. No Christian could do so without committing idolatry and thus found himself in the desperate position of having to defy public law as a matter of conscience. Indeed, it was more than conscience; it was love for God and obedience to one of the Ten Commandments. Thus, what the early Christians sought and needed was exemption from emperor worship, as well as the legalization of their faith. Their disobedience was highly specific and did not generalize outward into a broad rebelliousness toward all Roman law. It was a narrow need, but so vital to their good conscience that they died martyrs' deaths to uphold it. They were neither revolutionaries nor traitors nor insurrectionists. They were enveloped in pagan laws they surely considered unjust, laws that permitted all the pagan vices and lusts to flourish, but it is not recorded that the early saints sought to overturn the civil order. They were not subversives, although the governors of Rome regarded them as such. Rather, they sought to salvage the souls of men and teach the mercy of God. They had little to do with the imperial regime except when it compelled them to violate their consciences.

The point is that Dr. King's formula, taken literally, would permit civil disobedience only in instances where the law compels a Christian to sin. That, however, is not what Dr. King had in mind, nor is it what his followers and a whole generation of alienated idealists interpreted it to mean. What they meant and what they believed was that they could disobey any law they *disliked* or which they felt had a malevolent impact on some people. All this was to be determined, not by public standards, but by their own private opinions as to what is right and wrong. Such a viewpoint has no basis in Christian belief. It cannot be found in the teachings of Christ, not even in His generalized higher ethic of loving neighbors and enemies. It is to be found neither in the epistles of the disciples nor in the older Jewish law and tradition. No such anarchy of private will was ever contemplated by the Jews or received as prophetic law.

The irony is that in a narrow sense Dr. King was right: a public law that compels a Christian to sin before God must be defied. The higher law of doing God's will is the controlling moral imperative. Of course, such circumstances are rare; the state rarely imposes such conditions upon us, and usually the exercise of our free will will prevent us from falling into evil. Dr. King's formula was ultimately tragic; it embroiled the nation in instabilities and confusions of the heart that still echo sadly in the souls of our citizens.

V

Both St. Paul and St. Peter wrote extensively to the young churches under their wings, urging them to be obedient to civil authority. In a remarkable discourse on Christian obedience, the author of the letter of Peter urged both due respect for such pagan governments and proper obedience by slaves to masters, masters to God, and wives to husbands. All of which is indeed difficult for the modern mind to assimilate and accept.

What makes the whole business so striking was that the Christians were at that time undergoing terrible persecutions at the hands of the very rulers to whom Peter and Paul were urging obedience. One could well argue that the two apostles were merely being prudent, that such admonitions were bound to rest well with civil authorities who might thus ease their persecutions against the outlawed Christians who would not bow to the emperor. Such an argument must be regarded as suited for that circumstance and time and not for all the ages of Christianity to follow.

Much more than prudence was involved in such admonitions, however. It was an integral part of the young church's belief that civil authority had been vested in the Roman governors by God. This disregarded the fact that the emperors and their minions were pagans; it blinked at the corruption threading through their courts; and it ignored the persecutions of Nero and his successors that decimated the ranks of the believers and caused still more to defect and to curse Christ and kneel before the royal images.

The belief that such civil authority came from God was based on nothing less than the words of Jesus. The Gospel of John records that, at the time Jesus was brought to trial before Pilate, Jesus reminded the Roman governor that "you would have no power over me unless it had been given you from above. . . ." (John 19:11) This idea was consistent with the view of the prophets that God had on occasion delivered the people of Israel into pagan hands such as those of the Pharaohs or had otherwise permitted the conquest and enslavement of the Jews. In other words, neighboring rulers were sometimes seen as instruments of God. "Shall I crucify your king?" asked Pilate. "We have no king but Caesar," answered the high priests.

Peter may have witnessed these events; Paul surely heard about them. In any event, Paul exactly echoes Jesus in his letter to the Romans:

> Let every person be subject to the governing authorities. For there is no authority except from God, and those that exist have been instituted by God. Therefore he who resists the authorities resists what God has appointed, and those who resist will incur judgment. For rulers are not a terror to good conduct, but to bad. Would you have no fear of him who is in authority? Then do what is good and you will receive his approval, for he is God's servant for your good. But if you do wrong, be afraid for he does not bear the sword in vain; he is the servant of God to execute his wrath on the wrongdoer. Therefore one must be subject not only to avoid God's wrath but also for the sake of conscience. For the same reason you also pay taxes, for the authorities are ministers of God, attending to this very thing. Pay all of them their dues, taxes to whom taxes are due, respect to whom respect is due, honor to whom honor is due.

Thus does Paul ordain, not only obedience to the rulers of Rome, but also respect, honor, and taxes! Clearly, he commends more than a surly obedience, a grudging acquiescence. Respect and honor are elements of wholehearted support for magistrates. Paul's writings are a firm echo of the things Jesus said about the subject, and his views look forward to an era when kings would indeed be ministers of God, visiting God's wrath on wrongdoers. Significantly, too, he urges the Christians to be subject to rulers "for the sake of conscience." This whole discourse, in other words, sharply rebukes Dr. King's theory of civil disobedience for the sake of conscience.

At the time Paul wrote this he must surely have been aware of the corruptions and depravities raging through the pagan world. In fact, he explicitly enumerates them elsewhere. Still, he could find it within his spirit to describe the governors of that empire, then nearly at its apogee, as servants of God! If his words were inspired by the Holy Spirit, as Paul insists they were, then they must have been directed to a higher and longer vision than merely the current situation. One can guess that Paul was laying the groundwork for a revolutionary reform of the ancient world, in which rulers would for the first time be governed by the restraints of God, even as they governed. Even though the passage is addressed to the governed, it carries within it the understanding that governors were not a law unto themselves, that they were subject to God as much as were their subjects. In terms of the ancient world, such a concept was a radical and humane new vision.

The passage also was clearly consistent with Jesus' admonition to render unto Caesar what is Caesar's and to God what is God's, for in a good commonwealth obedience is the very minimum that is owed magistrates. A citizen is also obliged to pay due respect and honor to those appointed to look after the general interest and to pay taxes willingly. In a sense, however, this whole passage evades the problem of evil government, the problem that can be symbolized at the extreme by Hitler. Perhaps Paul believed that such evil would quickly collapse of its own weight or at the hands of God; in any case, there is little instruction about what a Christian should do if he knows, for example, that his ruler is murdering thousands of Jews in concentration camps.

The difficulties pile up. The remarkable aspect of this entire passage is that it supports the rulers and traditions which would ultimately lead to the martyrdom of Paul himself and which were even then spreading terror and havoc through the early churches and their timid, often humble, brethren. A little later, when Peter's epistles were probably written, it had become a capital crime merely to be a Christian, and the whole sect was widely considered to be depraved and cannibalistic, a misapprehension no doubt stemming from the Eucharist. One thing is clear: when the state demanded that which was due to God—that is, worship of emperors—the early Christians not only defied the state, but defied it even unto death. It is difficult to reconcile the idea that rulers are servants of God, exercising God's authority, with the idea that emperors declared themselves gods and demanded worship. In our own day Hitler came within an ace of declaring himself the high priest of a god called the Fatherland.

The difficulties can be partially reconciled through the realization that the state is not one, but many. At the time when emperors were proclaiming their divinity, competent and sober governors were still scattered through the empire. The procurators usually governed fairly, punished wrongdoers, rewarded good behavior, encouraged patriotism, and sought virtue and truth. The republican virtues of Rome were upheld firmly despite corruption in high places. Civilization rested on these lesser men even more than on the emperor. They were fine administrators who kept the peace and protected persons and property. The durability of the empire suggests widespread good government, despite the politics that wracked it.

The idea that rulers would eventually be Christianized and be subject to God's law, like other men, is evident in Paul's first letter to Timothy, in which he urges that "supplications, prayers, intercessions and thanksgivings be made for all men, for kings and all who are in high positions, that we may lead a quiet and peaceable life. . . ." (2:1) Thus does Paul envision, even amidst terrible persecutions, a day when the masters of men would be aware of their Master. In a letter to Titus he urges strict obedience, telling his colleague to "remind them to be submissive to rulers and authorities, to be obedient. . . . For we ourselves were once foolish, disobedient, led astray, slaves to various passions and pleasures, passing our days in malice and envy, hated by men and hating one another. . . ." Here Paul has included obedience to civil authorities in the context of a wholly disciplined Christian life as though obedience were a part of the seamless web that extends throughout a man's whole relationship to others. To be unruly toward governors, yet obedient to all the laws of God, was simply impossible, or at least improbable. Obedience was apparently regarded as a cast of mind that would govern a Christian's whole relationship to God, to the brothers in the church, to rulers, and to others outside the fold. If obedience to God was truly the important thing to Paul, then whatever strengthened that obedience to the Divine Will—including obedience to civil authorities—was perforce necessary and good.

The letters of Peter, which may have been partly the work of his followers, emphasize the same theme of obedience through all Christian life. "Be subject for the Lord's sake to every human institution, whether it be to the emperor as supreme, or to governors as sent by him to punish those who do wrong and to praise those who do right. For it is God's will that by doing right you should put to silence the ignorance of foolish men. Live as free men, yet without using your freedom as a pretext for evil; but live as servants of God. Honor all men. Love the brotherhood. Honor the emperor."

This passage obviously has prudential motives; such obedience would help stifle the misconceptions then rampant about the new church and would ease the persecutions. The author goes on to develop the familiar point that obedience is part of the eternal will of God. "Servants be submissive to your masters with all respect, not only to the kind and gentle but also to the overbearing. For one is approved if, mindful of God, he endures pain while suffering unjustly. . . . Likewise you wives, be submissive to your husbands so that some, though they do not obey the word, may be won without a word by the behavior of their wives, when they see your reverent and chaste behavior. . . ."

Here again the text holds out the prospect that obedience can be the means of converting pagans, whether they be masters of slaves or husbands of Christian wives. In fact, the church was liberalizing the ancient world's attitudes toward both slavery and marriage. It was the custom then to treat both slaves and women as chattels, and the church was rapidly altering those relationships. The apostles made it clear elsewhere that in Christ there were no masters and slaves or superior husband and inferior wife, but that all had equal access to grace. That view was so radical in the ancient world that the apostles were forced to move circumspectly. Rather than simply denounce the master-slave relationships, they began the great radical movement by reminding masters that they had obligations to their Master and reminding husbands of their Christian obligations to their wives. That obedience might be the avenue toward freedom and equality was a doctrine at once astonishing and bizarre, as much to the ancients as to ourselves. Still, an obedient Christian master must perforce consider and admire his obedient slave, and the slave's cheerful obedience could only awaken new fraternal feelings in his master. Likewise, a husband obedient to the new Christian law of love perforce came to regard his wife, not as a chattel, but as a sister in the Lord, while the wife could evoke new feelings in the husband only through her cheerful obedience. It was logical for the apostles to apply the same formula to the rulers of Rome. Strict obedience to the magistrates of the empire would, and ultimately did, open their hearts to the new faith, as well as to the rights and dignity of the governed.

It will always be a source of wonderment that the apostles could lay down a firm policy of obedience to governors at the very time the young church was being brutalized by one of the most terrible persecutions in recorded history. It was necessary for them to cast their eyes on horizons rather than upon the bloody struggles immediately at hand, and this they did without faltering. Armed with the inspiration of God, they turned obedience, one of the most hated of all virtues, into a cornerstone of reform. That the apostles could envision the fact that cheerful obedience would result in social freedoms, more equality, and the conquest of an empire by the new faith was simply miraculous. The pity is that Martin Luther King and his followers lacked the same perception, with the result that their course would only stiffen resistance rather than ultimately cause a change of heart in their oppressors.

The acts and records of the apostles furnish clear-cut guides on the question of civil disobedience. Where the state invades the prerogatives of God, it is the Christian's obligation to disobey; this was as true of emperor worship as it is now true of the Communist regimes that seek to abolish the church. To that extent, Dr. King's formula is valid. For the rest, the Christian's recourse and avenue of reform is loving obedience, a rule that is clearly laid down at great length by Peter and Paul and that has direct roots in the words of Christ.

VI

It is apparent that the early Christians adhered closely to the idea of rendering to Caesar what is Caesar's and to God what is God's. They could and did defy the Sanhedrin; despite floggings and imprisonment, they continued to preach their new religion in Jerusalem and in all Israel. Likewise, even though their sect was outlawed throughout the Roman empire, they endured and preached wherever they could. This was an instance of rendering to God the things that are His, and they would not permit the state to interfere.

It is also true that they were not revolutionaries. They did not seek to overthrow any secular regime; they sought only to practice their faith. In all else they were enjoined to be model citizens, paying taxes and honor and reverence wherever it was due. They acknowledged the authority of governors. St. Paul's behavior before various Roman proconsuls and Jewish rulers was the very model of decorum and courtesy. Unlike so many modern radicals who assail the authority of courts and governors—one thinks of the Chicago Seven—the early Christians obviously conceded the valid authority of those proceedings. The ultimate model of those facing trial was Jesus himself.

When Paul was testifying in self-defense before King Agrippa, the Roman governor Porcius Festus suddenly cried out, "Paul, you are mad; your great learning is turning you mad." Paul replied, "I am not mad, most excellent Festus, but I am speaking the sober truth." (Acts, 26:24) Thus did the aristocratic, intellectual Paul respond with courtesy and respect. Imagine one of the Chicago Seven addressing Judge Hoffman as "most excellent Judge" or even "Your Honor"!

It was not necessary for rulers to be Christian or even wise and good. The office itself was revered because it involved the important execution of the common weal. Bad men and good might successively fill that office, but they were all to be revered, especially the bad, because due respect had a meliorating influence on evil tempers, whereas rebellious spirits and confrontations only deepened the wickedness of the evil. It was the Christian insight to meet evil with good. Of course, in the case of good and wise rulers it was easier for the governed to honor both person and office.

This Christian formula produced innumerable martyrs, but ultimately conquered the ancient world and reformed it. One cannot wander through the endless catacombs of St. Calixtus outside Rome without coming to understand the patient and awesome courage of generations of early Christians who conquered with peaceful virtues rather than by arms and force. The process required more than three centuries. Men died martyrs' deaths long before there was the slightest evidence that the ruling authorities would relent and permit the faith to flourish. By the time of Constantine the essential victory had already been won: at every hand were new men, dedicated to cleansing their own moral and ethical errors, building a new relationship with others based on love, and demolishing the licentiousness of the pagan world.

Christianity has bequeathed us a heritage, not of rebellion, but of obedience and reverence for civil authority. That stark fact cannot be denied even by the most ardent disciples of Martin Luther King. The high-born St. Paul, in particular, propounded a doctrine of clear-cut obedience even to evil authorities who proscribed Christianity. Paul's doctrine went beyond civil authority: he was anxious to inculcate a seamless web of reverence that would include due respect for church authority, ancient custom, parents, and the heads of families. Thus, the humblest child would find himself obliged to his parents and neighbors and governors and church pastors and ultimately to God. The humblest slave would likewise revere all above him. At the same time, however, Paul's doctrine imposed equal burdens on all in authority: henceforth they would lovingly consider the needs of all their subordinates. Thus, we were bequeathed a formula for stable and serene nations, for governments checked by the superior force of Christian duty and love. Governments were not required to be good to command Christian obedience. Neither must the governed be virtuous and industrious to command the love and respect of their rulers. Christianity did not remove high and low, rich and poor, slave and free; rather, it bound all together with bridges of duty and love from caste to caste. Although there is no discernible egalitarian doctrine in the teachings of Jesus, the net result of his doctrine is to build bridges of responsibility both upward and downward, so that the poor and humble are cared for and respected and the rich and powerful feel heavily obligated to care for the less fortunate.

The tantalizing question is whether this ancient formula has validity today. In a fast, secular, complex world, is there much sense in the old Christian formula, especially one that prohibits disobedience and encourages reverence toward rulers? One has the uneasy feeling that the American Revolution, for example, lacked a basis in Christian example and teaching. King George may have been autocratic and a blunderer, but one can scarcely discern any authority in Christian doctrine for the rebellion. Still, one can scarcely deny the fact that the rebellion triggered the release of human energies and wisdom that built a nation of unparalleled magnificence, with unparalleled opportunity and liberty.

The question is not easily resolved. If so much good sprang from a treason with little Christian justification, does the old doctrine err or is it now irrelevant? Are there perhaps purely secular justifications for rebellion that are grounded in economic and political, rather than theological, values? The problem becomes even more acute in contemporary contexts. Civil disobedience has produced noticeable achievements in the form of jobs and integration for the blacks and sympathy in some quarters. Even student rioters on campuses have achieved evident results, including such dubious ones as coed dormitories. It goes without saying that the activists who set out to shred our judicial system have succeeded beyond all expectation. For good or ill, the system is gravely undermined. It is possible by piling up sophistries to reconcile ancient Christian obedience with modern disobedience. One could argue, for example, that the American Revolution brought about greater religious freedom in this country by eliminating the official status of the Church of England, or that it produced an egalitarianism toward which Christianity was already moving. One could contend that the civil disobedience of blacks merely accomplished in a shorter time what the older Christian methods were already approaching. One could suggest that modern protests and sit-ins and confrontations are simply shorter and more direct expressions of Christian love than the doctrine of obedience and that they accomplished Christian results by "humanizing" institutions.

These arguments are tendentious, spurious, and sophistic. It is not possible to reconcile modern civil disobedience with the methods of the apostles confronting their persecutors. The Boston Tea Party cannot be defined in Christian terms, although it can perhaps be justified on secular grounds. The harsh fact is that Christianity has little to say about how societies are structured, not a word about kings and governors, capitalism and socialism, redistribution, welfare, high or low taxes, democracy or aristocracy, schools, franchises, the rights of minorities, impeachment, elections, pensions, unions, or eminent domain. When Jesus denied his secular kingship, he expressly eschewed the uses of force and the reformation of the social order. When Pilate asked him if he was King of the Jews, Jesus said, "My kingship is not of this world; if my kingship were of this world my servants would fight, that I might not be handed over to the Jews; but my kingship is not of this world." Nothing could be a more forceful and express abandonment of politics and force or the restructuring of the secular order.

The main disjunction between Christianity and modern liberals rests squarely on that disclaimer by Jesus. He adamantly refused to become a secular king, even though in that position he could by liberal standards have created a sublime social order refulgent with justice, mercy, freedom, opportunity, piety, and virtue. It is this stubborn fact that damns liberalism and likewise damns all civil disobedience and power politics. Jesus had another avenue in mind. He sought the reconciliation of individuals with God through himself, the salvation of souls. As that was being achieved, more and more virtue would flow into this world in the hearts of individuals. The nature of institutions would ultimately be insignificant. Perhaps we can discern an operative principle from all this: the more virtue there is in the world, the less important are secular institutions, but the less virtue there is in the hearts of men, the more crucially important are well-honed institutions that substitute law and rights for love. Evil, rebellious, surly, suspicious, and greedy men need exact and massive rules and defined institutions to function in a civil society. Where love is operative, rules become less important: employers have a rich concern for their employees, and vice versa. The poor are spontaneously cared for; the courts are idled by the reconciling forces at hand. If all this is true, then perhaps we can see that secular methods achieve good only in a roundabout way because they fail to deal with the soul. The American Revolution did achieve things; so have the civil disorders of our own times. We need not suppose that nothing good came of all the troubles and tumults, but we should recognize that a Christian approach would have produced richer reforms with little backlash because change would have occurred within the heart rather than on the law books or in polemic literature.

Perhaps the best way to deal with such great politicosecular enterprises as the American Revolution, modern civil disobedience, or even modern liberalism is to recognize that they do achieve good results, even though they leave more negatives in their wake than did the ancient Christian method. In no way can they be reconciled to the Christian doctrine of obedience, and in all likelihood their militance and nihilism directed against established order spread the seeds of future revolt and disruption, whereas Christianity has less backlash. All the fiery sermons from the puritan pulpits of New England in the 1770s necessarily ignored St. Paul's calm approach to reform and the clear authority of his teaching. Likewise, all the fiery sermons of the 1960s directing young people and oppressed people to take to the streets if nothing else availed also necessarily ignored the clear teachings of the church through its long history.

Another possible approach to reconciling the apparent benefits that result from civil disobedience with the Christian proscription of rebellion is to say, with the author of Ecclesiastes, that there is a proper season for all things: a season for revolution, a season for civil disobedience, a season for obedience. It is probable that, had the early Christians been the slightest bit rebellious during the Roman epoch, they would have been slaughtered and the church simply exterminated. Their obedience in all matters except worshiping the emperor may have kept them alive in that season, while in our modern time our state tolerates a good deal more rebellion and defiance. One thing is certain: the doctrine of obedience to rulers, while important, is not the central doctrine of Christian religion. One can scarcely conjure up images of Hitler and Stalin without immediately assuming that there may be season in which a Christian must resist a state whose leaders are diabolical.

If there are proper seasons for rebellion, the business of acting upon them is agonizing. It was Jesus, after all, who laid down the doctrine that the authority of rulers derives from God; that doctrine was greatly reinforced by St. Paul. In our time Christians have been called on to face the question of Adolph Hitler. Was it with God's permission or sanction that such a demonic man rose to such power? Was it by God's sanction or permission that Stalin ruled or that in older times emperors spilled so much Christian blood? I prefer to think that the office—the emperorship, the chancellorship, the secretaryship—rather than the man is what requires respect and obedience. In any case, it is significant that the most important plot of any consequence against Hitler, the 1944 Generals' plot, was the effort of committed Christians, both Catholic and Protestant. So far as liberal ideologues are concerned, that whole episode is miserable and inexplicable because it upsets their categories and epistemology. The plot was evolved by (1) Prussian militarists, (2) Christians, and (3) political conservatives. There were exceptions, of course, but the bulk of the participants fit two or three of those categories. One of them was the deeply patriotic Admiral Canaris, head of the *Abwehr,* or military intelligence. He quietly circulated photos of the death camps among the generals. These were moral men: the prospect of treason pierced them, as did the oath of personal allegiance they were required to swear to Hitler. It was difficult for them to comprehend that the oath had been given under duress: anyone who refused would have become a nonperson. In the end, they perceived Hitler to be demonic and considered their own effort to be the will of God. This perception was primarily the result of their Christian faith during those times of horror. Their bomb exploded a few feet from Hitler, but did not kill him as planned, and the conspirators were quickly executed or imprisoned, martyrs to the enduring church of Jesus Christ. Perhaps they failed because God meant them to fail; perhaps God did not want assassination to be laid at the feet of the Christian church. A Marxist and atheist succeeded in murdering John Kennedy, while some Christian officers failed to kill Hitler. There are agonizing questions in it all.

Christianity, and Judaism before it, have always loathed rebellion. In fact, the entire Old Testament is an account of rebellion and disobedience before God. Adam and Eve, Cain and Abel, Noah, Moses, David, Saul—the story of the unruly, stiff-necked people of God stretches back to Genesis and forward to our times, encompassing the entire history of man's relationship to God. Sometimes it was the entire Jewish nation that rebelled, in which case it was delivered into the hands of its enemies. It is important to our understanding of Paul's admonition to obey pagan rulers to know that in the Old Testament the pagans were often God's instrument to scourge his rebellious people. Perhaps the early Christian church had to undergo its fiery ordeal at the hands of the Romans to emerge with the proper authority to lay claim to the allegiance of the world.

At every point rebellion and disobedience are abominated in the scriptures. One of the principal theses of the New Testament is not that Jesus was a rebel, but that the Scribes and Pharisees were rebelling against God's law of love, substituting ritual for compassion, and sacrifice for mercy. To romanticize Jesus as a rebel, when in fact his earthly life was devoted to reconciling rebel hearts with God, is completely to reverse the purpose of the incarnation. If Jesus was in fact a rebel who could now be the patron of all the rebellious enterprises of our times, how strange is his lamentation for Jerusalem: "O Jerusalem, Jerusalem, killing the prophets and stoning those who are sent to you! How often would I have gathered your children together as a hen gathers her brood under her wings, and you would not! Behold, your house is forsaken. And I tell you, you will not see me until you say, 'blessed is he who comes in the name of the Lord!' "

The obedient prophets who were sent to Jerusalem only to be stoned did not come to foment rebellions, disobey laws, organize marches, or stage sit-ins. They were not rebels, but reconcilers. Had they preached in the American South in the 1960s, they might also have been stoned or lynched, but not because they broke civil law or organized a political enterprise. They would have died because their message was unbearable to the stiff-necked rebels in that area who have yet to learn about love.

Among the many magnificent gifts the Jews have passed along to Western civilization and the world is their concept of magisterial law. The Old Testament is a litany of law, as well as a history of a people trying to evade, and then learning to obey, the laws and ordinances of God that had been received through Moses. These were laws that struck at the inner vices, such as coveting, laws that went far beyond mere guides to conduct. The prophets were sent, one by one, to entice and shame the Jews back home to their law, and out of that vast experience came a shared consciousness of what law is, what it can do, and how one may profit from obedience to it. By the time of Jesus, the problem had become excess zeal for the law, emanating from a burning, even fanatical, hunger to honor God by observing every last iota of the law.

No people have ever had so much experience with law or profited so richly from legal concepts as the Jews. St. Paul, drawing on his high-born understanding of the law—he was a Pharisee—formulated some of the most compelling, though difficult, arguments for obedience to law that can be found in the New Testament. Moreover, he was able to describe every conceivable rationale for disobedience and to deal with it successfully, often out of his own experience. So the Jews passed their understanding of the law on to Europe through the prophets, through Paul, through the Old Testament, through their own tradition during their dispersion, and, of course, through Jesus of Nazareth, who said He came to fulfill the law. That gift of the Jews, along with Roman legal concepts, now forms the base of our civilization.

VII

One of the most amazing paradoxes of our times is the fact that the liberals encourage civil rebellion while simultaneously promoting vast new government enterprises. Sample any of the guests at one of Leonard Bernstein's radical-chic parties and you will find support for Black Panther guerrilla warfare against our government, as well as support for any civil disobedience anywhere on the left, but also support for any expansion of the government's activities: socialized medicine, consumer legislation, guaranteed annual income, and child-care centers, ad infinitum. One wonders whether the real intent of the left is to tear down its own house, painfully erected since New Deal days. Do they secretly hate what they have created?

There are innumerable explanations, none of them very good. It cannot be argued that the disobedience was directed only against state and local governments, when in fact much of it was poured out upon the Federal establishment in Washington. Neither can it be argued that the disorders were aimed only at the Vietnam War policies of the government when in fact massive disorders were invoked against campus rules, welfare and racial policies, State Department travel rules, draft laws, defense research, and Congressional committees. The fact is that the insurrectionaries condoned by liberals have challenged Federal authority and policy on nearly every front and especially in the areas where liberals or leftists are proposing massive new Federal responsibilities.

Most liberals would explain the paradox as no more than a means to an end. Encouraging disobedience to law is merely escalating the politics of liberal reform. A riot or two is stimulus enough to force the passage of a bill; a tough march scares legislators into compliance. They resolve the paradox, in other words, by saying that it is a tactic in the service of an ideal. They do not really favor civil tumults as ends, only as means to usher in social programs.

That does not quite explain their behavior, however. One discerns a prevailing Zeitgeist in which there is enjoyment of rebellion, a sensual pleasure in defying the "fuzz," a lust for disobedience, a heady ecstacy in bringing the great authorities to their knees. Indeed, some of the riots of the 1960s were uproars in search of a cause, and sometimes the participants neither knew nor cared what was involved. At other times the entire rationalization for the tumults—one thinks of the Columbia University episodes—was constructed ex post facto, either during the riots or following them. There exists in civil disobedience the simple pleasure of tearing down the house. No matter how the liberals squirm, they cannot evade that reality or evade their guilt in encouraging that sort of nihilism. Nothing else could explain the hero-welcome and adulation heaped on the Black Panthers by Manhattan cocktail liberals.

I have often discerned nihilism walking hand in hand with liberal social programs, although I never quite understood why this should be. The liberal psyche is baffling. It is true that, the larger the government, the more likely it is to be oppressive, costly, and uncontrollable. Perhaps liberals are pretty much like the rest of us, simply reacting to their own constructions with dismay. The government of the United States has long since passed the point where people have any pride in, or affection for, it. We used to regard it as something marvelous, something different in the New World, a government quite unlike the rickety bureaucratic monsters of the old world or the despotisms of Asia. All that is gone, however: we perceive our government as a beast identical to the beasts of Europe, give or take a few bureaus. The limited government that once was our unique joy is no more. Nevertheless, while most people are simply resigned to it, they do not start or encourage uproars against it or advocate defiance of its law, as Hubert Humphrey or Adlai Stevenson have done. There is something else in the liberal temperament, something that wants to spit at God. Perhaps they are bedeviled.

The liberals' disdain for anything that smacks of patriotism is another facet of the puzzle. To the extent that liberals confess any patriotic feeling, it is directed toward American society and the American people, but never at the government. As for the rest, liberal civil liberties lawyers are diligently demolishing any last claim, such as loyalty oaths, the government can lay upon its citizens. One supposes that just the opposite would be the case, that with each additional service or benefaction provided by the government, the patriotic excitement of liberals toward their government would reach orgiastic levels. With literally thousands of services and benefits available for the asking, one would expect not only a rabid patriotism among liberals toward their own Federal creation, but among the beneficiaries as well. Such is not the case. Bitterness toward the government quickly outweighs any gratitude people temporarily feel upon receiving a new service. Did the Great Society evoke a new patriotism? Or the New Frontier? Is there now a true joy in our government among the mass of men or among the liberals?

It does not work that way. The more the government is bent to liberal specifications, the more surly they are about it. There is such a thing as hatred without a cause. We have a government that, despite its manifest failures, is generally benevolent. Its managers usually mean to do good and have high ideals. It does not have political prisoners. It permits the alienated to emigrate. It allows wide latitudes of speech and political organization. It permits the opposition to flourish. It is neither warlike nor imperialist, yet leftists treat it as though Hitler were in the White House, and George McGovern has gone so far as to make the comparison explicit. He only echoes timidly what is said boldly on the left.

At that great liberal center of learning, the University of Wisconsin, there is a plaque on the wall of one of the buildings on Bascom hill, a gift from a graduating class. It says, "And ye shall know the truth, and the truth shall make you free." It is a verse from the eighth chapter of the Gospel of John, and its sentiments are very popular among the leftist academics and students on campus. It is also the last half of a sentence, the beginning of which was carefully excluded from the inscription. The whole of verses 31 and 32 reads this way in the Revised Standard Version: "Jesus then said to the Jews who had believed in him, 'If you continue in my word, you are truly my disciples, and you will know the truth and the truth will make you free.'" If you continue in my word! If, that is, you are obedient, then you will know the truth and be free! It is not a formula the liberals can enjoy except for what they can take out of context. Jesus elaborated, saying "Truly, truly, I say unto you, everyone who commits sin is a slave to sin . . . So if the Son makes you free you will be free indeed." That is not exactly a liberal sentiment.

The assault against good authority on earth is a part of the rebellious spirit of those who deny and defy God. It is, as the apostles insisted, the same attitude that rebels against all ordained authority, including that of parents, church, governors, and God. That is what liberalism has now come to.

VIII

At the present time in the United States, a defined ideology of civil disobedience is not confined to the left. There is a similar doctrine on the right, marching under the flags of libertarianism. There are really two versions of libertarian thought, one with honorable Christian roots and the other totally corrupt and pagan in nature. Both of them seek the diminution of government, but only the corrupt libertarians actually hate the state and hate its laws and administrators. Only the corrupt libertarians defy the law and choose to be a law unto themselves in an anarchic fashion. The corrupt libertarians, naturally, have close ties to the New Left, and there has been a steady defection of these from right to left, epitomized by the odyssey of former Goldwater speech writer Karl Hess.

Liberty is not heavily stressed in the New Testament, although it is a valid Christian concept. It is often posited as the fruit of good moral order, not so much in society as in the personal soul. Freedom is primarily a matter of inner strength rather than the product of a mild government regime. To the extent that a Christian conquers his passions, overcoming his slavery to lust, laziness, greed, alcohol, and various idolatries, he becomes free. He can function in a wide variety of social structures—short of the totalitarian—as a wholly free man in command of his faculties and able to direct his will fruitfully and peaceably toward his goals. He is free in the capitalist liberal United States, in socialist England, in racist South Africa, in Greece and Spain, and even for the most part in Yugoslavia. He will meet with varying degrees of frustration and red tape in each of these milieux, but the essence of his Christian freedom is his inner strength, his ability to prevail in widely varied circumstances. This inner strength is the fruit of his faith and his morality; the idea is expressed in Corinthians: "Where the spirit of the Lord is, there is liberty." He has, in addition to his own strength, the power of God adding to his liberty, a power that opens pathways for him, a power that frees him even in rather oppressive circumstances. Thus, the libertarian Christian has no need to hate or defy the government unless it reaches totalitarian proportions. He is able to heed wholeheartedly all of Paul's and Peter's ordinances about cheerful obedience to the state, even though he may be deeply opposed to expansions of the state and its existing excesses, which he may see as being very damaging to the economy and to human liberty. However, a Christian is aware of the fact that his personal liberty is not ultimately rooted in the nature of government, but rather in his own character; his weaknesses and blindnesses are what ultimately enslave him and make him barren.

Corrupt libertarians, on the other hand, blame the government for their personal woes and thus evolve an active, intense hatred for and defiance of the valid magisterium of the state. If they are barren or lazy, they blame the state for "destroying incentive." If their business goes poorly, especially as a result of their sloth or incompetence, they denounce government intervention. No matter what their failings in business, creativity, marriage, parenthood, or social status, they ultimately lay the blame at the doorstep of the government and especially its taxing powers. Such an attitude is profoundly corrupt and is found primarily among the immature on the right or among the intellectuals *manqués,* including the Objectivists led by Ayn Rand.

Their notions are based on a rigid determinism or environmentalism that is almost identical to the determinism of behavioral psychologists, as well as that of routine left-liberals. The corrupt libertarian says, in essence, "The government made me what I am and is responsible for my failure and the failure of others." The political liberal says, in essence, "The environment made me and others what we are, particularly the unlovingness of the state, and therefore we must enact laws to change the environment." The behavioral psychologist, likewise, insists that human beings are molded by the environment and that man's nature can be changed only by altering that environment, mainly through the state. Thus in all three cases the nature of man is perceived as the result of an environmental determinism. Such a viewpoint is profoundly hostile to the Christian emphasis on free will and the capacity of each individual to sin, to gain virtue, and to achieve dominion over his life and nature. Corrupt libertarianism is thus secular and agnostic and looks to the state for solutions, namely the evanescence of state power. There is a patricidal overtone in that sort of thinking.

The corrupt libertarians almost invariably start to "kill" the state in their own minds by denying its authority over them. They perceive of rulers not, in St. Paul's words, as "the servant of God to execute wrath on the wrongdoer," but as personal slave masters who are themselves corrupt and illegitimate. The distorted nature of this sort of libertarian can always be seen in his embrace of base libertinism: the first laws he begins to defy are those governing morals. He casts aside legal restraints on, say, adultery or fornication or pornography and soon graduates to the more serious illegalities such as using pot or hashish or even the harder drugs, always justifying his deepening slavery to his sensual lusts and his defiance of government through the rationale that governors are not legitimate, but corrupt. So he becomes a law unto himself, an anarchist full of anarchical hatreds of valid authority, deeply twisted in his thinking, wandering down crooked and malevolent pathways toward the death of his spirit. The principal avenue of defection from the right has been over this corrupt libertarian bridge. Such "libertarians" give their hearts and souls to the Woodstock Nation, to the counterculture, even while retaining an intellectual link with the conservatives, whom they resemble less and less. In the end, however, they go to the other side, the secular and sensual side, because that is where their corrupt libertarianism leads them. They come to hate and defy the government while averting their glance from their own inner weaknesses.

They are invincibly blind. If they look, they will see at every hand, all through society, people whose incentive has not in the least been destroyed by the state: bustling people who work, achieve, suffer the pain and joy of creativity, earn, prosper, and advance. Despite this, these blind libertarians will insist that the state has already destroyed their own incentives, hopes, and dreams. The state has perhaps damaged the incentives of middle-income citizens, but not calamitously. To do so, it must confiscate wealth faster than real income is rising. Only in a period when real income declines continuously for several years, thus releasing deep frustrations and a sense of futility about work, will it truly erode incentive. Even then, however, men who are free in a Christian sense will not lose their fruitfulness. There is no hope for those who blind themselves so wantonly, and that is why, in the end, they become revolutionaries.

5

The Peace Conspiracy

Liberals were not exactly exasperated with Christianity; on the contrary, they are fond of most religion except when it interferes with their own superior attitudes. Rather, the ancient faith did not have quite the moral tone that modern standards require, especially on the question of peace, an area where church leaders have for centuries been ambiguous and sometimes openly in favor of war. Of course, most liberals have long since abandoned the church on just such grounds: their humanism could not be adapted to the church's ancient dogmas that involved a supernatural God and redemption from sin.

There was, indeed, ambiguity about war, and not only in the New Testament. In the Old, the entire history of the Jews is a chronicle of war, and much to the dismay of moderns the scriptures frequently insisted that God was leading the armies of Israel.[1] Even the commandment, "Thou shalt not kill," was disappointing because the original Hebraic word was murder, and that seemed to condone war. About murder there was never any question, not since Cain slew Abel. But war—well, those tribes were a very bloody people, and there is

---

[1] "When you go forth to war against your enemies, and see horses and chariots and an army larger than your own, you shall not be afraid of them; for the Lord your God is with you who brought you up out of the land of Egypt. And you shall draw near to the battle, the priest shall come forward and speak to the people, and shall say to them, 'Hear O Israel, you draw near this day to battle against your enemies: let not your heart faint; do not fear, or tremble, or be in dread of them; for the Lord your God is he that goes with you, to fight for you against your enemies, to give you the victory.' " (Deut. 20, 1-4)

"When you draw near to a city to fight against it, offer terms of peace to it. And if its answer to you is peace and it opens to you, then all the people who are found in it shall do forced labor for you and shall serve you. But if it makes no peace with you, but makes war against you, then you shall beseige it; and when the Lord your God gives it into your hand you shall put all its males to the sword, but the women and the little ones, the cattle and everything else in the city, all its spoil, you shall take as a booty. . . ." (Deut. 20, 10-14)

no lesson in it for secular moderns to whom war means something infinitely more terrible.

Even King David, from whose line the Messiah would spring, is recorded in the books of Samuel as a bloody man. He slew Goliath and then cut off his head, but God did not hold it against him. Further, before he became king, he and his private army swooped down on the Geshurites, the Girzites, and the Amalekites, "and David smote the land and left neither man nor woman alive, but took away the sheep, the oxen, the asses, the camels and the garments . . ." A king who visited such disasters on his neighbors would not endear himself to us today, but the scripture records that he was greatly loved by God and his people; indeed, the women used to dance before him, naming him "The slayer of 10,000 enemies."

So the Jews warred, and if one accepts the Old Testament as more than just myth, but Divinely inspired, one must accept the fact that they warred with God as their field marshal. Of course, they desired peace, and the days of peace, when there were no lamentations and ugly wounds and relatives eternally lost, were counted as treasures.

The Old Testament is dismaying to religious liberals, but they can scarcely do better with the New. The Prince of Peace is not recorded in any of the Gospels as discoursing against war or urging a pacific comity of nations. Also, what He said about peace was ambiguous: "Blessed are the peacemakers, for they shall be called the children of God." Peacemakers between what? Antagonized individuals? Hostile organizations? Opposed nations? It could be any or all of these, but given the weight of his other teachings, which dealt almost exclusively with the souls of individuals and personal relationships with others, He was probably talking about peacemakers who settle the ruffled feelings of other persons.

He said there would be "wars and rumors of wars" in the last days; that is, at the end of the epoch, so evidently He did not conclude that the church He would found would succeed in wiping out war. Neither did He supply any ideas about a new diplomacy or improved communication or a new world organization like the United Nations that might solve the perennial dilemma of war. Moreover, when He used the word "peace" it was usually in a personal context. He used the word to describe, not the relationships between nations, but inner unity and the tranquility of the soul, the condition of not being at war with one's self. He made himself very clear on that point just before He faced the cross. "Peace I leave with you; my peace I give to you; not as the world gives do I give to you. Let not your hearts be troubled, neither let them be afraid." In this context, peace has a very personal meaning. It is not something an ideologue at the United Nations would care much about. Elsewhere in the Gospel of John He uses the word even more emphatically as an inner tranquility: "The hour is coming . . . when you will be scattered, every man to his home, and will leave me alone . . . I have said this to you, that in me you may have peace. In the world you have tribulation; but be of good cheer, I have overcome the world."

St. Paul did no better to placate the secular left. His peace was also an inner unity, as for example in his letter to the Philippians: "And the peace of God, which passes all understanding, will keep your hearts and your minds in Christ Jesus." (4:7) There is nothing about international diplomacy in that. The verse is preceded by one about having no anxiety, and is followed by verses commending pure, just, honorable thought. Similarly, he wrote to the Colossians to "let the peace of Christ rule in your hearts, to which indeed you were called in one body." (8:15) Again, he is describing an interior peace.

St. James pursued the same theme, only from the obverse side, describing war as the result of lusts burning within individuals: "What causes wars, and what causes fightings among you? Is it not your passions that are at war in your members? You desire and do not have; so you kill. And you covet and cannot obtain; so you fight and wage war." (James 4:1) Thus, the fathers have plainly described peace and war as internal conditions springing out of the heart. It is a hard-learned lesson that is lost on many today.

It is puzzling to envision social circumstances, such as peace and war, as conditions that spring directly from the human psyche, yet that is essentially the teaching of the church fathers. There are, of course, intermediate steps leading to the organization of armies or the tranquility of nations. Organized ideologies usually convert private passions into public action. Nationalism, socialism, liberalism, anarchism, egalitarianism, monarchism, and conservatism can all be the catalysts that can transform private lusts, such as greed, envy, covetousness, egotism, vanity, vengeance, or paranoia into concerted action. Ideologues intensify such passions while politicians organize and manipulate those who have been saturated with ideology.

Christianity, as always, goes directly to the root of the problem: thus James does not bother with ideologies in his description of the causes of war, but strikes directly at the source. No derivative ideologies can spring up among a people whose hearts are peaceful. Christianity always deals with roots and never with intermediate stages, and that is why historians of the West are forever being led back to theology when they seek causes for the things that have happened since the time of Christ. It is not social conditions themselves that provoke war, although the liberals seem to think so.

Jesus had a chance to strike a blow at the existing military-industrial complex when a Roman centurion asked Him to heal a beloved servant. It was His custom to urge people to repent, to begin life anew, but Jesus did not urge the centurion to repent of his military ways; on the contrary, He praised the soldier for his remarkable faith, even though he was a Gentile. He did not say a word to the effect that soldiering is an evil profession.

Even more striking is an event described in Acts in which a Roman centurion named Cornelius and his family become the first Gentile converts to the fledgling faith. The story is important because it is clearly the will of God that this centurion of the Roman Cohort be made the first non-Jew in Christianity. First Peter has a vision in which God tells him that "what God has cleansed you must not call common." At the same time the soldier Cornelius has a vision: he is to send men to Joppa to bring Simon Peter to him. Peter comes, explains the new faith, and then a full pentecostal experience befalls them all, and the Holy Spirit seals their faith. The event is so God-directed, so otherworldly, so contrary to what the reluctant Peter desired or believed about the spread of the faith, that one cannot doubt that God chose a devout soldier as the first Gentile Christian, with a Divine purpose in mind. If neither Peter nor Jesus saw fit to condemn the profession of arms, one wonders on what moral grounds the liberals or the Fathers Berrigan see fit to do so.

If the Prince of Peace did not anywhere in recorded scripture condemn soldiers, however, that does not mean that peace was not his object. From the beatitude we know that peacemakers are sons of God, and we have that great commandment to love one's neighbor as an overriding law of the faith. Moreover, we have his great moral imperatives: turn the other cheek; love your enemies; do unto others as you would have them do unto you—all of these are paths to peace. Jesus was, as always, working toward that blessed estate in his own way. If the hearts of those who love God and their neighbors are peaceful, then, and only then, will nations also be peaceful. His was not the worldly wisdom of high diplomacy, but the simple and yet agonizingly difficult concept that real peace begins inside the heart and extends first to family and neighbors and employers and communities before it can spread to strangers and foreign countries. One can imagine a truly peaceful world only as one in which the peace of Christ controls the hearts of most of the rulers and ruled. The comity of nations is the final rather than initial step along the path of peace. We have seen such a peace rest serenely in many Christian mini-societies: some church congregations, some convents and monasteries, and some hierarchies. We have seen it work imperfectly, as well, especially where unchristian ideas are introduced or pagan hearts are poised for plunder. A guard against the unpeaceful people of the world remains a necessity. One cannot, after all, defend the West from Soviet tanks and rockets with a cohort of Quakers or even with a militia of Berrigans.

It is this reality that leads to the Christian ambiguity about peace and to the secular liberals' private scorn of the whole idea that Christian moral leadership will ultimately hammer swords into plowshares. There is in Christianity a strain of submission that would simply surrender to invading armies and then seek to civilize them, love them, and root out their lusts. However, it is not certain in Christian teaching that the idea of turning the other cheek or meting out good for evil is meant for societies and governments as well as for individuals; that is, whether it was meant for commissars who are intent upon extirpating from the face of the earth every last vestige of the Christian faith. It may be that doing good in response to evil is a profoundly valid and beautiful way for individuals to lessen antagonism in the world, but it is doubtful that such doctrines apply to societies or nations, which have no collective soul, but only many individual souls. We know that the idea is brilliant and workable on a private level: the soft, loving response to hatred over and over again astonishes and warms the heart. But would billets-doux have warmed the heart of Josef Stalin? Would submission and loving tenderness, as a diplomatic ploy, melt the ice with Kosygin and Brezhnev? One can entertain some doubts without courting heresy.

Although the word peace is used overwhelmingly through the New Testament to connote a tranquil heart, there is here and there the usage that is closer to what the liberals mean by it. St. Paul's letter to the Ephesians contains such a passage about amiable relationships between peoples, but even that is not what secular men might expect. Paul reminds the Ephesians that "you Gentiles" were once alienated from God and from Israel, but with the historic appearance of Christ things were changed. "For he is our peace, who has made us both one, and has broken down the dividing walls of hostility, by abolishing in his flesh the law of commandments and ordinances, that he might create in himself a new man in the place of two, so making peace, and might reconcile us both to God in one body through the cross, thereby bringing the hostility to an end. And he came and preached peace to you who were far off and peace to those who were near. . . ." (2:11) Here St. Paul describes the reconciliation of alien peoples, Jews and Gentiles, in and through the church. Indeed, he goes on to describe the unity of all in the church. Clearly, the word peace does have to do with hostile nations, but the method of peace—bringing warring peoples into the body of Christ—must dismay those secular souls who continue to seek pacifism in Christianity. Thus, once again does the faith disappoint the moderns who expect to find a solution for war through diplomacy within it. The solution is there, nevertheless, but not in any sense that secular men will accept or even understand. It rests on the acceptance of Christ.

The faith's historic involvement in wars and especially fratricidal conflict is still another mark against it for those who are impatient with the world as it is. Much blood has been shed in the name of Christ, particularly between Catholics and Protestants. In addition, there was the war of some centuries' duration against the Moors of Spain and the several crusades against the Turks. The crusades were wars of aggression rather than defense of a homeland, although Jerusalem was the spiritual homeland of Christians everywhere. Such wars directly expanded what was to be known as Christendom. Was Spain to be Christianized in any way other than the patient southward pressure of Christian kings? When Ferdinand and Isabella finally ejected the last of the Mohammedan rulers from Granada in 1492, it was the culmination of centuries of effort spurred on by the beatific vision of a people redeemed. It was certain that no meek and mild turning of the other cheek would ever—no, not in a thousand years—seduce the fanatical caliphs to abandon their own allegiance to Allah. It was either clear Europe of the heathen by force or not at all, so the warfare between the faiths lasted into the 20th century. There were wars and crusades, some fanciful and foolish, others the work of clear-eyed kings and queens, of whom Spain's great Isabella and Ferdinand were the most brilliant.

Thus, the history of the church dismays liberals, who note how rarely it has taken a clear stand against the shedding of blood. While some attribute this to the worldliness and corruption of the church, they fail to see that the very doctrine of the church has such ambiguities embedded in it, questions that reach back to the apostles and to Jesus. The Christian belief in an afterlife somewhat mitigates the horror of bloodshed for the faithful: however terrible pain may be, death is not so frightening or dreadful. The prospect of heaven has strengthened many a Christian heart on the very eve of battle. Some of the carnage of the centuries, death upon death, is thus transmuted into sacrifice for the faith, a building process that would permit the church to function peacefully behind walls of safety. If war was death, there was also the prospect that in a Christian war new souls would come into contact with the faith. If Christian arms could secure the temporal world, then eager priests and, later, ministers, could convert the vanquished peaceably into the great unified church of Christ.

It was not that war was a specific instrument of the church, but rather that it was sometimes inevitable, as when the Turks were piercing deep into the heart of Europe. The church always perceived itself as being in the world, though not of it. Being in the world necessitated some politics and sometimes that extension of politics we call war. The war mutilated men, widowed women, orphaned children, and caused pain and suffering and insanity, but it was somehow akin to the suffering of the Prince of Peace, and it was felt the end justified the means. It is not that Christians historically favored war, but that they were forced to resort to it. It is not that the apostles or their successors taught war, but that war injected itself into all generations. The church taught a doctrine of love, a divine love that could heal the tormented nature of man and fill individuals with a peace and love that could translate ultimately into international peace. The true army of Christ did not carry swords, even if temporal rulers fought with swords on behalf of the army of Christ. So there were wars, sometimes with each side unfurling the banners of the cross of Christ. These were tragic wars, but conflicts perceived as the defense or advancement of the holy faith, wars that surely grieved God, but battles waged so that love might reign on earth and men might have hope. Was it all senseless and wrong and unchristian? It would be easy and facile to say yes, but there is always that disturbing reality that God arranged for the Christian faith to be brought to the Gentiles through a centurion named Cornelius.

It is clear why secular progressives prefer to place their hopes in their own peace machinery such as the United Nations, the World Court, and sophisticated diplomacy. They want some machinery operating that will eliminate war. Their trust is invested in institutions and engines of peace functioning with sovereign authority over all nations rather like a godhead of mankind. Christianity was not good enough for them; its methods of creating peaceful hearts was too roundabout and devious. War had been denounced from time immemorial by the church, and the ritual incantations against it by a few nasal preachers were scarcely a guarantee of peace. What the liberals wanted was something concrete with which to replace God. The old myths could then be retired. Men might consider them relics of semitic tribal life but scarcely the moral force to halt war in the brave new world. Rational men were compelled to fashion their own peace scientifically with the knowledge and techniques at hand, which is to say, out of international law and arbitration and all the other concepts that Eleanor Roosevelt and her people relied on as the sole hope for man.

The problem was always more complex than the progressives imagined. Mature Christians recognized that something was missing from such machinery, that all those blueprints for an international order were devoid of the love that began with God and radiated through the whole church, imbuing it with light and authority and with the actual power to change personality. World peace would not arrive or stay for long without a preliminary change in the inner personality of many men and especially their leaders. Love is not a common phenomenon among statesmen. This was not an idyllic or beatific vision; a loving personality was a practical necessity for peace in the world. There must first be peace with God and one's self and then with spouse and children and neighbors. Was it so idyllic to insist that this humble peace was the sine qua non of a grander peace among nations? Machinery had rarely worked, but love had sometimes succeeded. It was love, Christian love pouring out through God's grace, that would create the environment for peace, for love lessens envy and selfishness. It reduces fear and overcomes hate. It changes piracy and plunder into peaceful trade. In a world where there are only marriages of convenience among nations, the unity of the universal church provides the bonds of peace. This is true even if there have been wars among factions of the church. The expansion of the church with its emphasis on brotherhood and all the fraternal values is the sure and steady path to a tranquil world. There are no shortcuts. Alliance and détentes are tactics for the moment and not strategies looking toward a world that is comfortable and secure. Whatever the church's failures may have been, it remains the doorway to peace. It alone put first things first.

II

The United Nations was a surrogate for God, although none of its liberal and establishment proponents saw it that way. For them it was "the only hope for peace," with emphasis on the "only." They saw no other way. It was created because secular men believed that God had failed. They could not see the connection, and they did not seriously consider the sort of peace, described by St. Paul, that results from the universality of the church and its brotherhood.

It was a liberal assumption that if nations would at least sit down and talk to one another—the favorite word was "dialogue"—there would be a relaxation of tensions as each side began to understand the other. From dialogue would come understanding and then the softening of hostilities and then the appearance of good will and compromise, and thus peace would be spurred along. In addition, the UN would formulate international law so that there would be guidelines, and there would be a world court to interpret and apply them. Its potent authority would rest on the assent of nations and ultimately on a UN police force. Sanctions would be applied collectively to aggressor nations. Thus, if the instrument could not exactly hurl Jovian thunderbolts from the clouds, it could at least seduce and ostracize.

The dream was never really implemented, despite an occasional minor success. The great powers scorned the instrument, preferring to deal among themselves. For the Soviets in particular, the UN became a propaganda sounding board. The dialogues occurred as planned but, to the dismay of those who had such faith in them, intimacy of understanding resulted more often in stark and hostile disagreement than in reconciliation. Communication, it turned out, was as likely to heighten tensions as relieve them, especially when the hidden intent of the Communists was to stir up trouble. To the extent that the peacekeeping mechanisms worked at all, it was in such lesser conflagrations as those in Palestine or the Congo. In the Korean situation the UN was technically involved in a grand alliance against an aggressor, thanks to the departure of the Soviets and their monotonous veto for the duration. The major burden was borne by the United States, however, which was itself hamstrung by political limitations on the degree of victory that it could achieve.

In time, the peacekeeping machinery was virtually abandoned, and the enterprise was turned into a debating society under Third World auspices. It functioned rather well in that capacity, providing a forum for the multitudes of lesser nations to vent their hatreds, envies, and hostilities, which are as numerous as the grains of sand on a beach. Moreover, the technical divisions of the UN involved with health, welfare, economic progress, and questions of maritime and international law did achieve a certain usefulness, sufficient to preclude abandonment of the enterprises. If the great godhead envisioned by Eleanor Roosevelt-type liberals turned out not to be divine because it was divided against itself, at least it could be a clearinghouse for African and Asian rhetoric.

It is ironic that just about the time that the last hopes for actually achieving world peace through the UN withered, the Communist Chinese were finally admitted to membership. Their entrance—their newfound legitimacy, so to speak—thus amounted to nothing at all, rather as though Harvard University admitted everyone and passed everyone and graduated everyone. As one of the great powers with Security Council status, the Red Chinese role would be to agitate Third World causes in an organization that has not been able to do much else for several years. Their victory was Pyrrhic, as was the American liberal victory over those who preferred that Red China remain ostracized. After all, it was the liberals' principal argument that the Red Chinese must be admitted so that their hostilities and sense of isolation might be mitigated and bent to peaceful purposes. As long as the UN was puissant, it was at least a logical argument, if one set aside the fact that the Red Chinese had behaved in a manner in violent conflict with the express ideals of the charter. And so the liberals achieved their victory just at a time when it made no difference. The charter had been debauched previously by Soviet intransigence, by India's aggressions and hypocrisies, and by assorted African wars waged by peace-loving African democracies. To include Red China in such company was simply to acknowledge one of the family. The only things still operative in the charter were the mechanisms of organization.

The UN might have had a better time of it if it had been an organization of Europeanized nations from the Americas and Europe. Such nations would have shared enough bases, including language and religious traditions, as well as Western concepts of rationality, at least to comprehend each other. However, the UN was grandiosely conceived to embrace the whole globe, from mini-states in the Indian Ocean to Mother Russia. Further, it was grandiosely conceived as a means by which bushmen who might yet worship snakes and fear ghosts and toads might commune with technicians and scientists intent on the laws of physics. It was partly the unconscious desire to replace God that motivated the founders to wish to include every last soul in mankind. A logical god is after all pantheistic and universal. It would have been more rational to include only those nations that shared enough common tradition to achieve some basic goals and to exclude the rest. The Third World bloc now sloshes through the organization, slopping its hostility here and there, not in accordance with such rational principles as nonaggression, but on behalf of tribal loyalties. Thus, South Africa is solemnly declared an aggressor, along with Rhodesia, although neither has invaded or threatened anyone, but a dozen African democracies that habitually inflict war on their neighbors are never denounced for their "peaceful" forays. Such nations defy Western concepts of sovereignty, and their proliferating presence has only served to turn the godhead into a wastepaper basket. It is a handy place for leftover problems. The motivating force of the Third World is never peace, but the exploitation and embarrassment of the great powers.

There was a time when the American left, and especially our liberals, sought to create a single world army: a UN peacekeeping force that was to be coupled with the disarmament of all nations. The theory was that the single army, under the rational and benevolent direction of the noble executives of the UN, would quickly squelch any nascent war before it attained global proportions. Jove was to be equipped with thunderbolts. The idea has vanished into the thick of the night, and one finds only embarrassment among those who conceived it. The problem is: who in the UN would control such a monopoly army? The very idea of a single unopposed army—a monopoly of power and coercion—roaming freely anywhere on earth, unmolested except by a few police forces and unbalanced by countervailing power, is monstrous on its face. The competition for control, the plotting, assassination, schemes, alliances, treachery, bribery, graft, corruption, and naked lust that would be unleashed for the control of such a glittering prize would quickly shatter the UN and create the causes for nuclear war. The possibility that such an army could be used by the poorer countries to plunder the wealthier ones would generate a ferocious politics. Such a monopoly army would be the most glittering, glistening, and evil prize in the history of man, the object of every looting spirit and avaricious nation on earth. In the hands of Marxists it would unleash the ruination of the world economy and reduce all human liberty to that enjoyed behind the iron curtain. If it is true that the excessive power of the American Presidency has evoked the violent, byzantine politics of Watergate, then how much more violent and vicious would be the politics surrounding an unopposed world army?

The fact that such a monopoly army was seriously advocated by sophisticated liberals, abetted by the tiresome world federalist types, is macabre, the waltz of ghouls. It may well be the ultimate insanity in all Western history, a madness that makes Marxist delusions resemble children's fantasies. It takes only a primitive understanding of the nature of man, whose virtues are counterbalanced by greed, rebellion, and lust, to perceive that the effort to establish such an army is the effort to enthrone the Prince of the World and to overthrow God. What is carefully excluded from the liberal equation is, in theological terms, an understanding of original sin. Man can not possibly be governed by himself alone, but only by a transcendent authority, because only God is good. Not even a UN filled with saints could prevent such a monopoly from looting, pillaging, and inflicting death.

If such an army chose to invade the United States on some pretext or other—

the powers of invention are limitless—our disarmed republic would be raped. There would be a reign of terror: confiscations, mass murder, and infinite heartache. The evil prize of global domination would kindle lusts so relentless that most of the world's population would die in the struggle. Nevertheless, this was a serious liberal proposal, discussed at chic cocktail parties.

What is puzzling is the left's visceral allegiance to the scheme. It was something felt and desired, but never thought through. It was something grounded in an unquenchable thirst for anything that could replace God. Even as the apotheosis of the UN never quite happened, despite the best efforts of Norman Cousins to entice the heavens to open up and a golden shaft of light to pierce down on the UN building, neither has its theology ever quite taken hold. Since it was an article of faith in the best liberal menageries that war was rooted in poverty and colonialism, there was an army warring against colonialism from the beginning, with liberal philosophers playing the fifes and drums. It succeeded amazingly well. The European powers surrendered their possessions one by one, except for a few strategic tidbits here and there. Portugal was a lonely exception, clinging stubbornly to its colonies, with the hope of ultimately giving them equal status with the home provinces, rather like Alaska and Hawaii. By and large, the world is now free from Western colonial rule, although Communist imperialism continues its expansion.

The new republics have swelled and divided like amoebas, and we keep track of their number only by examining the UN rosters periodically. If the trend persists, the organization will be compelled to build an annex. In dark Africa, the multiplication has scarcely been a source of peace. Indeed, since the departure of the colonial powers, tribal wars have decimated whole populations, hundreds of thousands have been slaughtered, and even larger numbers have been dislocated or have seen their property confiscated. At present, General Amin's Uganda is the main culprit, but next month it will be another African empire. There were, of course, occasional colonial wars between imperial powers, but the impact of most colonialism was to secure peace, halt tribal conflict, and permit the development of large native populations. Colonialism wrought its evils, but war was not normally among them.

When the colonized populations established their independence, the general result was economic decline, the return of war, the loss of freedom, and even the onslaught of starvation. This was less true in places like India, where there was an advanced civilization to fall back on, but in Africa independence was a disaster. One thing is certain: independence was never a formula for peace. History has never been the strong suit of the left. If the new nations turned out to be bloodstained, that was no reason to exclude them from the grand structure of the UN. Eventually, the Third World will perhaps devour itself, especially if it has ample small arms, and move us all toward peace by wiping itself out. In recent years the liberals have ceased to support black Africa and have even grown skeptical about India. Instead, liberals have been making war against unborn babies, which is more satisfying because their victories are so complete and final. It is strictly a democratic war, waged against fetuses without regard to race, creed, color, national origin, or previous condition of servitude. To the extent that liberals form a separate nation within the West, they fit exactly into the

Third World. Perhaps some day soon the United Nations will recognize the sovereign republic of Liberalism, which is even now a kingpin of anti-colonial forces dominating the UN.

The UN is at its best performing missions of charity and technical aid. These provisions and experts, usually supplied by the United States, have saved lives and strengthened Third World economies, but their impact on world peace has been negligible. Not even the Peace Corps, building village wells, improving agriculture, and teaching children all over that world, has pacified it. Neither food nor economic growth seems to induce peaceful hearts. Food itself is rarely a cause of war, except in certain African areas where the losers supply protein to the victors. War is rooted principally in passions and lusts, the chief of which are aroused by ideology or religions. Not all the foreign aid that could reasonably be supplied by wealthy nations could forestall war; it might simply provoke conflict. Material abundance fails to abate tribal hatreds, religious antagonisms, and the competition of diverse economies. A great many wars are fought for no particular reason: they simply occur, and rationalizations come later. In the advanced and civilized West we insist on reasons, but there may be none among the actual participants. Not even ancient tribal hatreds fully explain these sporadic and spontaneous eruptions. The wars arise spasmodically from some dark atavistic part of the soul, a rage against life itself. To ascribe rational causes to war is to misread the character of mankind and to ignore the mentality of primitives. War is not a phenomenon that can be dissected easily in liberal drawing rooms or in the theses of Ph.D. candidates.

The UN, however, should not be denounced by every skulking antiintellectual. The intent of its creators was to save mankind from further bereavement, and that goal is honorable. It quickens any heart. There is scarcely a family on earth that has not suffered loss or death or privation through war. If there had not been a cold war, if Karl Marx had never written his Manifesto, perhaps the UN might have had a slender chance to operate a global federation, but that was not to be. However idealistic its founders may have been—and idealism is not something to be casually scorned—the concept faltered when reduced to reality. The cosmic vision, the macropolitics, all turned out to be less practicable than, say, regional defense treaties such as NATO or economic integration such as has been achieved by the Common Market. It was idealism, but an idealism of despair and illusion. It was to be the fount of world law, and it did indeed spill out a great deal of law. Nevertheless, it also spewed out a lot of politics, as well as defiance of those very laws by powers that never grasped the true nature of law or what the UN was intended to achieve. The very idea of law means one thing to Western man and quite another to an Asian or African. Even in the West, Anglo-Saxons perceive law in a different light from the French or others whose law is Roman in origin. If there is such difficulty with law even within the West, how much more difficult is the case in which law is perceived by wholly different civilizations?

The UN was originally conceived in Western terms; its charter exudes a Western rationality. Its goals are Western, and its divisions of power imitate Montesquieu. It has, however, evolved into a club that exudes the rationality of Asia and tribal Africa, the logic of the Third World. It is not the goal of the lesser nations to create or impose peace among the great powers or to generate a body of international law and morality. Those are all Western ideas. Rather, the Third World seeks to build alliances, punish and isolate such enemies as Israel, blackmail the great powers, and deepen racial antagonisms toward all whites. There is no place in all of this for the Western idea of building a great supranational organization that would exercise moral force, demand obedience, create law through precedent and arbitration and legislation, and ultimately reconcile hostile peoples. The organization has moved along its own tangent as the liberal European prestige within it has diminished. Thus, the liberal visionaries, the poor Eleanor Roosevelt cabal, were betrayed by the happenstance of Third World renaissance, a world that anticolonial pressures created and nourished. The UN nevertheless exists, and it should continue to exist for good or ill. Ideally, the whole enterprise should be turned over to the Red Cross.

III

The American peace movement crested in the 1960s at about the time when most rational men gave up on the United Nations. The peace lobby was, of course, hostile to an American presence in Vietnam, but it did not seriously appeal to the UN to take action. The UN was dead by then, which made the peace project seem all the more desperate and desolate to those who participated in it. By the same token, neither did the United States government make any sustained effort to turn the war against North Vietnam into a UN effort, even though there was demonstrable aggression by the north against the south. There were ritual denunciations of the war by U Thant and his colleagues, but nothing ever came of them.

The peace movement was not composed of pacifists, by and large, although there were a few such genuine pacifists as Quakers among them. Numerous motives undergirded the entire enterprise, but the thread that bound them together was the remoteness and unimportance of Vietnam to American interests. It was difficult for the government to justify such an incredible expenditure of blood and treasure for a small, distant, tropical Asian nation. Sensing this irrationality, the peace movement seized upon apparent petroleum prospects in the Vietnam area as the real reason—in essence, an imperial war—hiding behind routine anti-communism. When this proved to be illusory, if not fantastic, the idea evaporated. It turned out that anti-communism was, after all, the central reason for the war, which may be why there is such a revisionism about the cold war among liberal historians and journalists. In any case, the government's reasoning was circular: we had to pursue the war to maintain our credibility as a deterrent force against aggressors. We were fighting to prove we were serious. To make the argument all the more circular, we were fighting to protect American troops. Occasionally it was mentioned that we were also there to protect the freedoms and lives of the South Vietnamese, and especially those millions who had fled from the tyranny in the north, or that we were there to fulfill the terms of the SEATO treaty. It was never very clear that United States interests were directly or substantially threatened, certainly not to the extent that it was worth over $100 billion plus about 50,000 lives and countless wounds. It was, at best, a valid rationale for technical assistance and limited logistic help such as was successfully supplied to Greece and Turkey by the Truman administration after World War II.

So the peace movement had at least one solid argument: we had drifted into a war the costs of which were all out of proportion to our national interests and security, even in the context of the cold war. This argument was greatly strengthened by the decision of three administrations to treat North Vietnamese territory as sacrosanct; no matter that the north was the aggressor, we would not invade that country or seek the security of the south by capturing the war leaders in the north. The government thus telegraphed to the American people its own uncertainty about the war and its own feeling that the war was not terribly important. We would not destroy Ho Chi Minh as we had annihilated Hitler or Mussolini; we would not invade Hanoi as we had once attacked Berlin through the West Wall, and the Siegfried Line with every resource we could muster. It was not urgent that we capture Hanoi. Thus, the peace movement was conceived and grew in the very womb of the government's policy of a semi-war, half fought. Because of the total commitment to victory in World War II, no peace movement existed; it could flourish only in the fertile ground of uncertitude. In the early stages of the Vietnam war, a total commitment and decision to capture Hanoi would have quickly silenced the peace movement. A truly mobilized nation has no room for pacifists.

So it was always easy to oppose the war, and even rather chic to do so. Mr. Gallup was always able to ask the questions that would have been unthinkable in the midst of World War II. President Johnson's addled policy of incremental escalation—telegraphing our intent in advance—also contributed to the peace movement by ensuring a war of attrition with maximum bloodshed and no visible exit. The constant vacillation about bombing and targets was still another goad to the peace movement. If the President was unsure whether it was right to bomb, then the war itself was suspect. Although President Johnson professed virtual idolatry for Franklin Roosevelt, he apparently never grasped the fact that Roosevelt would wage total war, or no war at all. F.D.R. did not wring his hands publicly about whether to invade Germany, attempt to capture Hitler, or whether some areas of Germany would be bomb sanctuaries, or some might be civilian, and therefore not targets. The peace lobby eventually destroyed LBJ, mainly because he could never bring himself to choose between waging the war he had escalated to major proportions, or retiring from the conflict.

To all intents and purposes, the liberal Johnson and Kennedy administrations had invited the peace movement to exist and flourish. President Nixon did not invite it, but was hamstrung by it. He inherited a situation in which that movement was powerful enough to limit his options. That he was able to extricate America, free the prisoners, and achieve at least a brief hope of freedom for South Vietnam was a remarkable feat that combined brilliant diplomacy with bombing and mining pressures that sent the peace lobby into a total frenzy. By the time Nixon came to the White House, the peace lobby had expanded to such proportions that it was even furious with the President for successfully withdrawing from the war. It had enjoyed its supermoralist role and now found itself without a war to inveigh against.

The most obvious reality about the peace lobby is that it failed, even though it had some fairly solid arguments with which to oppose the war. The net effect of all its activities was to prolong the bloodshed by preventing the government from moving decisively and by encouraging the North Vietnamese to believe American will was faltering. It might once have been possible to win the war quickly by using decisive force and capturing Hanoi or it might have been possible for the United States to withdraw unilaterally, but the unfortunate tendency of the peace lobby to march with Vietcong flags and to denounce American "imperialism" made such a withdrawal politically impossible. To appear to kowtow to the lobby on those terms was political suicide. The lobby's open and ardent support of the Viet Cong simply destroyed any prospect it had of being an authentic domestic pacific force. To insist that the United States was guilty of war crimes while saying nothing about North Vietnamese atrocities; to demand the impeachment of the President; to claim that the war was motivated purely by capitalist and imperialist reasons; to contend that the North Vietnamese were innocents being victimized by our military-industrial complex—to insist on all this was to stiffen the administrations as well as the rest of the American people against any precipitous withdrawal.

Peace is not built upon accusations, but upon reconciliation. In the entire history of the peace movement, there was scarcely any effort to reconcile anything, least of all the North Vietnamese to the south or to Americans. Certainly, such a reconciliation was not achieved by Jane Fonda broadcasting diatribes from Hanoi, by Ramsey Clark's accusations against many Americans of good will, by screaming riots at the Pentagon, or by publishing hate literature against Presidents Diem, Ky, and Thieu. Reconciliation was not what most of the peace people had in mind unless reconciliation could be interpreted as widespread recognition that America was totally in the wrong and Hanoi entirely right. Reconciliation does not seek scapegoats, targets, and enemies. Peacemakers do not vent unstable emotions and hatreds in riots, threats of impeachment, and treason. The reconciling spirit begins with Christian love toward all, a love that questions the warlike policies of both participants and sympathizes with the victims of both sides.

Of course, there were some among them—the pacifist clergy, in particular—who sought true peace and prayed for peace, who lived according to the beatitude, and believed that reconciliation required cooperation from both sides. Many of them had not prayed for peace during World War II, but rather for a speedy victory and the safety of our boys. For mysterious and unfathomable reasons, they became pacifists and prayed for peace in the Vietnam war, perhaps because it took much less courage to be a pacifist. Maybe it was because they did not believe in the rectitude of the American effort; if that was the case, then they were not so much pacifists as doubters who thought the North Vietnamese might be in the right. A true pacifism does not spring from such doubt, but from a desire to reconcile through love. All too often, the peace movement cloaked itself in the aura of great moral purpose and lofty intent when it was doing nothing more than venting its spleen. There was nothing essentially moral, even in a symbolic sense, in burning draft cards or pouring chicken blood on draft records; the intent was to outrage public opinion rather than to heal divisions among us.

It is significant that a cease-fire was achieved only after two great events: the American people resoundingly defeated the peace movement in the person of George McGovern and President Nixon launched unusually heavy bombing raids directly against Hanoi in December 1972—two sticks and no carrots. Until then, the peace feelers and talks and accommodations offered by three administrations had been scornfully rejected by the north, which had plainly placed its hopes in the success of the American peace movement in weakening the American will to fight. Until the movement was rebuked or about to be rebuked, there was no prospect of peace unless the Americans wanted to pack up and abandon South Vietnam to its fate.

If the peace movement had not been pro-Hanoi, but had been deeply oriented around the idea of halting aggression, the talks might have succeeded much earlier. Its thrust, however, was never toward peace. Instead, it attempted to demonstrate that (1) the government of South Vietnam was illegitimate, undemocratic, and corrupt and had a weak hold on its people; (2) the North Vietnamese were invincible, modern, strongly supported by their people, and had history on their side; (3) the war could not be understood in terms of Communist aggression, but only in terms of Asian resentment against white imperialism; indeed, that Ho was an Asian Tito, independent and nationalist; (4) the United States was not fighting from high motives, but with an imperialist and colonial intent; and (5) our side was guilty of massive war crimes, inhumane warfare, and endemic atrocity. Thus, it was a Hanoi party rather than a peace party. There was never any serious effort to persuade North Vietnam to desist or withdraw to its own territory, no moral pressure against Vietcong atrocities. The entire weight of the movement was directed exclusively against the American role and was aimed at creating doubts and confusions about our mission and blackening our ally. The campaign was successful beyond anything ever seen in this country; it was as if the Nazis had successfully persuaded us that they had a divine right to Europe and that the conquered countries were so corrupt as to not be worth the struggle to free them.

A bona fide peace enterprise would have been possible only within the confines of an earnest patriotism. It is perfectly possible to support the flag without supporting the war; to seek peace without offering aid and comfort to the enemy; and to admire the gallantry of our soldiers while seeking to halt the bloodletting. But virtually from the war's inception, the peace activists supported Hanoi. Suspiciously early, they claimed they had exhausted all democratic avenues and were compelled to resort to illegal or extralegal methods to make their case. In fact, they scarcely tried to promote their peace lobby through democratic means, run candidates, hold forums, or write letters. Discovering that they were a minority, they rejected majority rule and set out to cow the majority with violence. Their excuse was always suspect because the movement took to violence from its inception. All this is not to say that there were no attempts that stayed within democratic boundaries; there were in fact continual sporadic efforts. There was nevertheless an unwillingness among the radicals to organize a political party on peace terms. Significantly, the organization finally came about in 1972 after years of uproar had failed. Nearly a decade after the peace movement had begun to create civil disorders, it got around to organizing the capture of the Democratic Party and running George McGovern. The Mc-

Govern people of 1972 were the very ones who staged uproars at the Pentagon in the middle 1960s, claiming that violence was their only recourse.

It is axiomatic that a peace movement must not supply aid and comfort to an enemy that would encourage it to keep on fighting or to believe that it will triumph. Thus, it was the first and most crucial task of the movement to discourage Hanoi's aggressions, to develop a peace faction in the Hanoi government, and to let Hanoi know that winding down the war by the United States would require reciprocal reductions by the North Vietnamese. With its intent thus clearly expressed in terms of peace rather than anti-Americanism, it could have developed its arguments against both the United States and Hanoi leaderships. Since the American intellectual mystique is built upon alienation from society rather than on support for it, a peace enterprise was perceived only in terms of pouring out venom against the ruling party in this country. Perhaps the one authentic pacifist in the war, the one with no hatred for either side, was Pope Paul VI.

The encouragement of a peace faction in Hanoi was not beyond the realm of possibility, even in a Communist country. In fact, the American radical left had access to Ho, and could have used its good offices to dissuade Ho from his imperial war, which was spreading far beyond the confines of Vietnam. Instead, it encouraged the north to fight. It is not recorded that Jane Fonda ever encouraged her hosts to live in peace with their neighbors; neither did the peace faction ever dispute North Vietnam's claim to be the rightful rulers of the south. There were pacifist protests against North Vietnamese aggressions, but these stand out historically as isolated incidents that ran counter to the flood of pro-Hanoi sentiment in the movement. It is perhaps true that the war could have been terminated four years before President Nixon ended it, but that would have required that the Hanoi party abandon its efforts to sabotage majority sentiments. It was necessary to signal Hanoi.

Peace is ultimately based on love, and that includes a loving respect for our leadership. A peacemaker's understanding and gentle persuasion at work on all parties was a necessity. The key to peace was to be able to love Lyndon Johnson and understand his view, to love President Nixon and encourage him with hope and support and concrete options. So long as there was not an ounce of charity, not a drop of mercy, not an iota of compassion, and a deliberate effort to misunderstand by ascribing the basest possible motives to all these Presidents did, the peace movement was itself playing out the role of a Hanoi column in enemy territory. It is so easy to accuse and so hard to reconcile that perhaps it was no wonder that the holier-than-thous took the road they followed. Out of their hatreds came a war of attrition, unendingly bloody, with the hopes of a small nation fueled day by day by internal disorders across the great Pacific. These were not the sort of peacemakers who could ever hope to become the children of God.

IV

Part of the reason the peace movement failed so miserably was that it was grounded less on love than on terror. Death lurks in silos and bomb bays, turning even small wars into events with terrifying potentials. The terror was so pronounced that Senator Goldwater could not even discuss the possibility of defoliating the Ho Chi Minh trail with tactical nuclear weapons without suffering a landslide of panic. The terror of nuclear death has produced serious kinks in the postwar generations, and these sometimes operate in ways to heighten rather than lessen the prospects of war. They were certainly all manifest in the peace movement, bared nakedly amid the hatreds vented against the Pentagon and the government. They were the rationale, for example, for not invading the north: to do so would somehow trigger the dreaded big war by involving Red China. It was never very clear just how that would happen or whether China would risk a confrontation that might endanger its revolution. The watchword was escalation. It was felt that escalation would unleash the terror, and that would be the end of the world.

The motives of most of those in the peace movement were not particularly pacific. Some dreaded death. Others hated conscription and military life. Others loathed the United States or Middle America and actively sought its embarrassment. Others were simply Marxists and favored the triumph of any Communist enterprise. Still others were intellectuals who put a premium on dissenting. Others were neo-isolationists who saw the Asian war as an unnecessary burden, as a thief of domestic progress. Some libertarians saw the war crisis as an excuse for aggrandizement of the executive branch. Others regarded the war as the creature of the hated military industrial complex. Still others perceived the war as a white man's aggression against all people of color. Some saw it as a degenerating force upon morals and ethics, but out of all this polyglot motivation that undergirded the peace movement, the weakest, most fragile strain was a true hunger for peace. Most of the real hunger came from outside the movement: from POW families, clergymen, and loyal middle Americans who had sent their sons to war with prayer and pride. It was this group that perceived that peace must come from both heightened pressures and reconciliation.

A single concept permeated the entire peace movement: the United States, being guilty of war crimes, imperialism, bullying, and excessive hubris, should pull out unilaterally. That viewpoint extended even to casualties of war. The movement had tender concern for the victims of bombing and for North Vietnamese families, but not for South Vietnamese, not for the grieving families victimized by Vietcong guerrilla atrocities, and not for our prisoners. They ranted against My Lai with fiery rhetoric, but rarely condemned tens of thousands of murders by the Vietcong. More than anything else, this monstrous selective compassion bared the Hanoi sympathies of the movement. Hanoi was a brave little nation fending off a white racist colonial superpower. The persistence and depth of that viewpoint, which extended even to a sputtering hatred of the released prisoners of war, suggests that peace had little to do with what was called the peace movement.

There was always a good case against American involvement, a case resting upon our actual strength and limited resources, the obscurity and distance of Vietnam, and the possibility that guerrilla activity would continue there, no matter which side won. Walter Lippmann developed that argument best, and his was an argument that emerged out of a deep love and loyalty for his country and an understanding of the limits of American power. I am not arguing that he was right, but rather that he was loyal and that his counsel gave little comfort to Hanoi. He was not a man who hated presidents. He knew who the aggressor was. He never glorified the North Vietnamese; he simply argued that the war was not worth the sacrifice.

It has been widely asserted that the war had a devastating impact on American life, introducing disorders, moral decay, corruption, and personal despair. The charge is valid to a degree, but it must also be recognized that the peace movement must share the guilt with the war. It knowingly and willingly fomented disorders, condoned immorality, and bred hatreds. Its fruit was the prolongation of battle and a fearsome bitterness and distrust of all public men. The very fact that a major section of the American people hated their republic and wished a defeat upon it suggests that much more was involved than the war itself. All this is not to exonerate the war, which had its own terrible impact, but to pierce the hypocrisies of a movement that blamed everything except itself. The peace movement demanded that the country be united; journalists and scholars wept over the divisions among us. It was impossible for Middle America to coalesce around a pro-Hanoi movement; simple patriotism forbade it. If there were divisions, the peace movement itself had produced them by being pro-Hanoi. It could not be assimilated into the national life.

It is a Christian insight that it takes peaceful hearts to form a peace lobby. When future historians study the fulminations of columnist Anthony Lewis of *The New York Times,* the salient pattern they discover will be a rancid hatred of American leaders rather than any deep hunger for peace. The same could be said for several other hate-saturated writers who were more interested in our "war crimes" than in negotiations. In the end, their truculence only encouraged Hanoi to continue to fight. So venomous was this gaggle of scribes that, when Mr. Nixon achieved a cease-fire, they hated him all the more. Their assessment of him had proven wrong; their image of him had gone sour. What was worse, the Thieu government had survived, and so they felt vaguely cheated. What they had lusted for was a great American humiliation, a Dunkirk followed by a war crimes trial that would have strung the President to the gallows, followed by General Westmoreland and General Abrams. It is simply not possible for souls harboring such bile to contribute to a real peace. They may capture all the Nobel prizes, but they did less for peace than any obscure housewife who prayed each day for the end of war. It is sad that there were no true saints during the whole period, neither a San Fernando to lead the war nor a saint to end it. The best that a man of God could come up with was soaking draft records in chicken blood. It was a gesture quite devoid of grandeur. It did not catch the moral imagination. Least of all did it reveal any concern for several million Catholic refugees who had fled North Vietnam, where their religion jeopardized their lives. The chicken blood trick was on the same moral and emotional level as the rhetoric of the peace movement. It was only another way of screaming "fascist" or "war criminals" or "genocide" or "racist" or "murder." It was part of the language of protest, rhetorical H-bombs dropped routinely upon our national leadership, language that Spiro Agnew in his wildest moments would never dream of emulating. The peace movement sprung rivers of bile that cut acidly into American life. If it in turn was accused of dubious allegiance, it had certainly invited the accusation. It left nothing luminous or inspiring, not even a striking discourse on the evil of war. It left no insight into the causes of war; no understanding of our role in the world or of a proper policy for Asia.

It is, of course, unfair to indict the entire peace movement. Many of the youngsters within it had nothing more in mind that halting a war they hated, halting pain and death from a war whose rationale they never understood. They sang peace songs that evoked a hunger for a tranquil world where they need not shiver with the fear of fire storms and radiation. There were prayers and vigils, and some of them were concerned about the prisoners of war. They wanted a world in which the sun would rise on peace, a world of ease and brothers and laughter and love. They marched through the night with candles, carrying their flickering hopes before them, and they were no one's dupes or fools, although in time they spoke the language of the Hanoi lobby and had less and less to say about peace. They were the sensitive and kind, Christians and Jews, the ones who could not bear to kill an ant, and all mixed up with an unholy alliance of leftist radicals, diabolists, drug cultists, and polemicists. The innocents were soon spattered with the Amerika-hatred of the others, and their virginity was lost. So the movement spread like the dark of a moonless night, with only a few twinkling stars to relieve the inkiness of the Hanoi lobby. Each time a vibrant lad full of hopes was converted into a Hanoi lobbyist, a star went out; by the end of the war the night was black, and the movement began a goblin dance on the grave of America. Somewhere along the way most of the activists who began as sincere pacifists changed into werewolves whose true goal was to see the republic suffer boundless humiliations. So it ended with a whimper and a whine and a feeling that Mr. Nixon had betrayed them because the peace was the result of stalemate rather than loss. South Vietnam lived. Marlon Brando couldn't stand it.

V

The best hope for peace in our times is not the United Nations, but something much humbler and more practical, something that would compel a drastic evolution within the Soviet and Chinese spheres. A massive East-West trade could have an incalculable impact on peace. When the business of nations is business, their warlike instincts recede, and barter becomes the coinage of diplomacy. Such universal free trade cannot be achieved without a massive increase in economic literacy; nonetheless, it offers the best chance to undermine Communist regimes with minimal damage to ourselves. It is a chance for peace, for ending the cold war while improving conditions behind the iron curtain. Such trade would not cause the overthrow of Communist regimes, but would result in a creeping capitalism compelled by the need to compete with the fecund Western economies, all of which would gradually heighten the ability of Soviet citizens to resist the state and to win some civil liberties. The whole idea is still taboo among conservatives, who have been so obsessed with what the Communists might do to the West under free trade circumstances that they have failed to consider what dynamic capitalism might do to the archaic and anachronistic economies of the Communist world. (I am not arguing here that communism can be liberalized or softened by modifying its ideology. This will be evident below.)

We do not have many options in the cold war. The possibility of a military first strike is foreclosed, not only by our national ethic, but also by the considerable superiority of the Soviet strategic force, with a megatonnage and delivery capacity manifestly superior to our own. War, while thinkable, would snuff out all the lights in the Northern hemisphere, and no man would want to carry such guilt in his heart—if he survives. On the other hand, if we foment internal resistance with the hope of gaining internal concessions for Soviet citizens, but stop at something less than revolution, the likelihood of savage repression, extending far beyond the historic liquidations undertaken by these regimes, would be very great.

If we foment revolution, a take-over by military units and an underground, not only do we automatically trigger a major civil war among those war-weary peoples, but an international nuclear war as well when the Kremlin strikes back at foreign intervention. Before the French revolution had run its course, it sent waves of death crossing and crisscrossing most of Europe. To ensure the absence of war, there must be simultaneous coups in Moscow, the satellite capitals, and perhaps even Peking.

We cannot hope to liberalize the regime or change minds within it. It is fanatically imbued with a secular religion that brooks no deviation or revision of its dogma. All other ideologies are heresies that can no more be fitted into Communist metaphysics than Buddhism can be fitted into Christian theology. The liberalistic notion that the Communists can be induced to see the light through dialogues rests on a misunderstanding of the dark forces that grip the Soviet leadership, forces that compel the most rigorous orthodoxies even in the face of shifting world conditions.

On the other hand, if we do nothing, we pass the initiative to the other side, at a time when its dynamism is increasing and its military strength is second to none. Containment does not really contain; it merely permits erosions of the free world. If we negotiate treaties and détentes, advancing here and retreating there, we are really elaborating the containment doctrine and therefore doing nothing. Diplomacy is at best a tactical-technical weapon and not a strategy with which to cope with a resolute Communist geopolitical drive that aims at global mastery.

The remaining substantive, rational option is massive trade, conducted on a broad scale, which the Soviets do not really want because it means loss of internal control. A modest, selective trade would not do the job because it would not generate forces within the Soviet economy. A broad trade effort could pierce the iron curtain and unleash forces in the Soviet economies that would require endless adjustments, forces that do not seem subversive to the commissars because there would be no ideology connected with them and no politics involved in them. Their bureaucrats would regard such forces as impersonal because they seem to have the deterministic qualities with which they are familiar in their Marxist-Leninist dialectics and that would require merely technical, but not ideological, decisions. These forces would shift the ground under them without altering their ideological imperatives. In a sense, such free trade would alter the reality of life in the Red-dominated nations. If central planners decide to give more autonomy to a Soviet washing machine plant to permit it to compete better with Maytag sales in the Ukraine, for example, the decision would have only the barest ideological significance. Free trade would not only unshackle the Soviet economy, but would also trigger vast economic longings among the mass of Soviet citizens, hungers for cars, motorcycles, tape recorders, outboard motors and boats, and all the astounding array of goods produced in the free world. To meet that demand, the Soviets would be compelled to export raw materials and reform their own economy to compete with the flood of American finished goods.

So the question here is not whether the regime can be liberalized, but rather whether it can be undermined so that forces are unleashed that compel the restitution of private ownership, a market economy, and natural inequalities. The role of the economic planners would perforce diminish. The nature of the choices open to the Red hierarchy in such a situation would be practical, pragmatic, and not ideological. It would not face the problem of subversion. The idea could succeed only if both the United States and the free European nations insist that such trade be broad in scale and open, and adopt that concept as their basic strategy. The Soviets rely heavily on certain Western products, such as computer technology, and this dependence provides the leverage to force the trade doorways open wide. It is along this broad, peaceful avenue that the cold war can be resolved without vaporizing most cities in the Northern hemisphere. The icons of the Soviet state religion would remain firmly emplaced, even though there would be a growing private sector counterbalancing Soviet political power within the iron curtain countries. Surely, that possibility is worth more serious consideration than it has received heretofore from American conservatives.

Most conservatives have rejected the idea in the past for good and substantial reasons, the most important of which is that trade could strengthen the grip of the Red regimes over their peoples. There has, nevertheless, been inadequate consideration of the impact of a deluge of consumer goods upon Soviet citizens, followed by Western advertising, repair services, sales representatives, the hunger for a better way of life. A crucial objection has been essentially symbolic: to do business with such murderous regimes is to sanction them, tacitly to approve of all the misery they have fostered. Alas, the argument is simply too late. Détente, massive wheat sales, and now an understanding with China have all rendered the old symbols moot. With the Soviets buying $2 billion worth of wheat and applying for favored-nation status, the argument no longer exists. Another objection involves subversion. While it is true that the MVD would discover opportunities in trade, it has never lacked opportunity in our open society and has effectively catalogued our installations long since in a free land where it is not unusual to wander around taking pictures. On the contrary, the prospect of admitting hordes of American businessmen to the Soviet closed society, where Americans have never traveled freely, poses far greater risk to the Soviets. An expansion of trade would affect their security far more than ours, although warming relationships brought about through trade might well eliminate any need or desire for intelligence.

A grave objection centers on the ability of the Soviets to use their controlled economy to ruin ours or, at least, to undermine strategic industries and resource extraction, for example, by dumping oil. The fear is that the Soviets could wipe out industries by undercutting prices. The result would be increasing dependence on Soviet natural resources or manufactures and a loss of strategic power. With an economy that does not function through normal cost-accounting decisions and in which political considerations override concepts of profit or loss, it would be possible for Soviet technicians and managers systematically to undercut the United States. The fear that this might happen has beclouded the realities. Not even the Soviets can suspend the laws of economics. They cannot sell oil at a loss to us long enough to damage our oil refining and retailing and drilling without doing themselves damage. A free economy is remarkably flexible and adaptable. Such competition, rather than killing industries that function in a market milieu, often forces them to compete better and to achieve new efficiencies. Moreover, technology has greatly multiplied the possibility of substitutions of both materials and processes. In a free economy, shortages are dealt with easily: if truckers are on strike, railroads, cars, buses, barges, and company-owned trucks are available. If copper or steel are in short supply, remarkable new plastics and alloys fill the gap. In an advanced manufacturing economy using the entire spectrum of new technologies and widening alternatives, the sort of trade sabotage that the Soviets might attempt would have minimal results and would likely boomerang by involving the Soviet government in heavy costs. In any case, the threat Soviet trade might pose to our strategic power is infinitely less than the impact American trade would have upon the entire Soviet economy and political structure. If the Soviets want foreign exchange to buy our products, they must improve their own sales, and they can do that only with radical economic reforms based on decentralization.

So the problems for ourselves tend to evaporate. On our side, the opening gambit would simply require the invitation to buy, the lowering of tariff and quota barriers, and the arrangement of credit. Far more difficult would be the effort to open up the Soviet Union to trade. We have a ready market for their raw materials, and they have a market for our finished goods, but their government's fear that a flood of goods would erode the power of the Communist state is well grounded, and they would wish to proceed slowly, if at all. Despite our high labor costs, our entrepreneurs could sell better products, shipped all the way to the interior of the U.S.S.R., at lower cost than Soviet goods, a reality that could improve living standards there, which would in turn relax the regime. Assuming that the door to Soviet trade can be pried open by degrees, the chance for breathtaking new opportunities to bury a harsh communism would unfold. The regime would survive despite the new relaxation and rising living standards, but it would be transformed. There would still be May Day parades, but the marchers would be employed in a quasi-capitalist economy. They might still visit Lenin's tomb, but not to worship. The flood of Western influence and goods would transform Soviet communism into the Yugoslav variety, and ultimately only the major heavy industries would remain socialized.

Such East-West trade would not necessarily guarantee peace, but it would help. The prospect of an evanescent communism wrought by massive trade offers the best hope of peace. The impact of such American marketing techniques as self-service groceries and filling stations, coin-vending, product guarantees, and advertising would compel remarkable change throughout Russia. Of course, such an end result could be achieved only by overcoming the economic illiteracy in both nations, especially the fears that trade would demolish local industry. Imports do that on occasion, but trade usually creates new industry and new jobs in the process and raises living standards as well. Cheap imports are not something to be dreaded by governments, but welcomed as a chance for better living standards and new jobs. The market place is the natural counterbalance to state power; the more the Soviets can be enticed into trade, the more they must relax their controls. The existing centrally managed Soviet system is so brittle that it could not withstand the dynamism of capitalist free trade. The import-export business would soon be punching wide holes in the iron curtain.

Trade is one type of transaction that benefits both sides. There is a pernicious mythology that it benefits only sellers, that buyers are disadvantaged by it. In reality, any system that permits buyers to obtain the highest quality at the lowest price raises their living standards. For this reason, trade is a natural, easy avenue toward peace. It does generate some resentments, but more often it creates easy camaraderie and alliances of convenience. By itself, the social contact engendered by trade builds peace. Virtually everywhere in the world traders are met joyously with the anticipation of mutual gain. Where there are social fractures and schisms, they usually run along trade barriers. The most vivid and valid description of the iron curtain is as a trade barrier. The soldiers who mass along that curtain are there primarily to inhibit free trade. Wherever the barriers are knocked down, as within the common market, the peace prospects between the trading nations are usually improved. Wherever the barriers are raised so that nations attempt to create private trade empires, political tensions reappear. Likewise, where nations attempt to achieve economic autarchy, they resort to measures characteristic of Nazi Germany, where Hitler was a great advocate of an autonomous economic empire. On the other hand, wherever nations have lowered barriers, permitting cheap imports even to the point of diminishing some domestic industries, the result has been a shift toward a cosmopolitan peace. Sometimes that competition is painful, but the overriding benefits lead governments to accept the decline of some less competitive industries so that others may advance. Low trade barriers help establish wage equilibriums and thus minimize disparities of income between nations, which are provocative when have-not nations grow envious. Any nation seeking peace need only open its markets to imports. The odd, almost paradoxical, thing is that it will flourish by doing so. Only its high-cost or inefficient domestic manufactures will suffer.

The good will generated by free trade can be converted into concrete peace by a good diplomacy. That good will builds ties that are not easily ruptured. It builds contacts that dampen hostility and strengthen peace. Trade is therefore a means of liquidating the cold war on terms acceptable to the West, as well as to the people of the Soviet Union. Communist dialectics advocate the use of trade to wipe out capitalism, but the reverse is the more likely prospect, as archaic collectivism gives way to free trade.

VI

Free trade is the foundation of peace and the great opportunity to win the cold war, but more is required. There must be growing trust and love, without which trade degenerates into a thieves' market, a Casbah of the corrupt, with black markets, smuggling, cheating, counterfeiting, and an endless variety of theft. Trade requires honorable traders, even as good diplomacy requires honorable national leaders and diplomats. A single national leader with an instinct for territorial aggrandizement or a paranoic fear of neighboring powers can upset the world's peace. The Thomas Eagleton affair during the 1972 campaign pungently demonstrated the dread people have of entrusting decisions in a nuclear age to anyone but the most serene and untroubled of men. It is not that Eagleton was unstable; it is probable that he had overcome his difficulties before the vice presidency was offered to him. Rather, it was that the public was in no mood to risk the possibility of an unstable man as commander-in-chief. The control of madness in high places is a technical problem for all governments that can be handled in a variety of ways, depending on the democratic or authoritarian institutions at hand. Beyond the technical problems there remains the overarching need to develop serene leadership that will respond slowly to provocation. This requires a wholeness of personality, a completeness of spirit that is not often evident in politicians. Governments such as that of John Kennedy, that arouse an excitable populace, that thrive on crisis and feverish, frenetic activity, that seek confrontations, that promise everything and then try to deliver it, are stark menaces to peace. It was no accident that a whole cluster of nuclear crises, ranging from the Berlin confrontations to the Cuban missile crisis to the Vienna summit— which drew us perilously close to nuclear war—were the result of an unserene administration intent on impressing the world. The peace of God scarcely existed or was remembered in jogging Washington, and the very concept of a serene government was regarded as a distasteful relic of the hated Eisenhower years. The Johnson years were not much better, although President Johnson was more relaxed than his predecessor. It took the first Nixon administration to restore serenity and to cool the hotheads that had been shredding the republic.

Thus, the Christian approach, creating first an inward peace and ultimately a world peace based on the inner tranquility of numerous people, is suddenly and starkly revealed as a necessity in our perilous times. It is neither a luxury nor a roundabout way that can be short-circuited by diplomacy between great powers. It is not something metaphysical or a toy of the theologians. There simply cannot be peace among leaders with stormy hearts, miserable suspicions, and unchained hatreds. It is a matter of first things first, the soul and the heart before nationalism, the building blocks before the building.

Of course, the simple acceptance of traditional Christianity is no guarantee of inner tranquility. Not even the saints quelled the wars within themselves. The towering St. Paul described his bitter struggle to impose his will on the rebelliousness of his flesh and noted despairingly that his will did not always triumph. Still, St. Paul and a host of other saints were peaceful men who controlled their passions more successfully than others. Through the ages, there have always been myriads of anonymous Christians who have achieved miracles of inner unity, however imperfect, that were visible to the world as profound love. There was peace, after all, amid their struggles because in the end God supplied it. The Christian formula for a tranquil nature is precise and clear: an absolute faith and love of God; the disciplining of the flesh and all its hungers; forgiveness as well as repentence; and love flowing in a gentle stream toward friends, neighbors, and strangers. The Good Samaritan was a peacemaker, as well as a charitable man. To the extent that men recognize such personal goals and begin modifying themselves to meet them, they will be doing more for peace than all the United Nations ever created. Peace is a gift expressly offered by Jesus Christ to all who accept him.

If it were necessary for all men to have peaceful spirits before there could be global peace, there would be good reason to despair. In fact, even a minority of calm and serene people can stay whole mobs, cool inflamed passions, calm nations, and reconcile the embittered. There is something infectious about a calm man who has surrendered all his anxieties to God and who can spread his tranquility and radiate his calm, even when beset by demagogues and the rages of tyrants. The magic peacemaker is even now present wherever the church exists, even behind the iron curtain. Such men are a natural part of the faith, an adjunct to Christian religion. They are not numerous, but they exist and should be encouraged to speak up. One thinks of Pope Paul as such a charismatic man of peace, but the bulk of such men are anonymous. They do not work at the grand levels of international diplomacy. They are not Henry Kissingers, but simpler souls who labor in humbler vineyards, healing frictions between husbands and wives, parents and children, minorities and majorities, whites and blacks, Republicans and Democrats, Catholics and Protestants and Jews, labor and capital, and a whole array of greater conflicts and sorrows. These priests of peace, unsung, unknown, unsupported and known only to God, daily build and rebuild the bonds that keep great civilizations from flying apart. It is always a tentative seesaw battle, with the salients and sectors changing daily. Wherever these humble ministers go, they build the promised peace of God, the peace that begins in homes, in bedrooms and kitchens, and then stretches upward and outward to the clasped hands of world leaders.

An Afterword

The thrust of this book has been to divorce Christianity from liberalism, to cleave traditional Christian doctrine from theological and secular leftism. It is clear to me that collectivist doctrine does violence to the faith and cannot be reconciled with it. Its means are not Christian; neither are its goals. While it operates on the fringes of Christianity, deriving some concern for the dispossessed from the towering charity of the church, its employment of the state to resolve all human difficulties, its belief in equality, and its schizophrenic pacifism-cum-war, all depart from Christian tenet.

I believe, in fact, that socialism is a species of idolatry in which the state is the godhead. The various brands of Christian Socialism share a tradition of twisting and torturing Christian doctrine to make it fit their ideological imperatives. If the reverse were true—if secular socialist doctrine were twisted and tortured to fit the immutable doctrines of the church—we might be dealing merely with a cult, an odd sect, an egregious error. On the contrary, we are dealing with an effort to portray socialism as the end, the fruit, the utopian result of a church established two millennia ago. We are dealing with an effort to portray Jesus as a social revolutionary, a rebel against his society, a leveler, a secular king, a misogynist, an ultrapacifist, and indeed a pre-communist, when through teaching and example He rejected all of these things.

In short, Christianity and socialism are not cousins, but enemies. The one is a secular political enterprise that employs government coercion as its motor. The other is a religion, concerned above all with the relationship of persons, of souls, with God. Despite the fact that both the secular and theological left express some responsibility for the deprived and seem therefore to be benevolent, the fact remains—on the basis of massive scriptural evidence, as well as centuries of teaching by the church—that the dogmas of the left have little in common with the dogmas of the church. Make no mistake: leftism is a dogma with as great a hold on its proponents as the sacred doctrines of the church have upon the faithful. So powerful is this secular dogma that it regards any reforms that do not spring from the godhead state as demonic.

133

The Christian Socialists have been astonishingly successful. Among the mainline Protestant churches it is surely the case that a majority of the faithful, including most of the clergy, believe that intimate ties exist between collectivist and Christian ideas and that the religion is "progressing" toward a saintly socialism. The National and World Council of Churches are structured squarely on that viewpoint. The Roman Catholic Church seems to be less infected, although it is increasingly besieged by packs of worker priests and gaggles of silly nuns spouting New Left slogans. In both Catholic and Protestant dominions, the lay congregations seem to be more orthodox than the clergy. Many pastors earnestly believe that a Christian who opposes state welfare—for example, one of the poverty programs—is guilty of a most heinous sin springing from a frigid heart and wanton selfishness or perhaps from diabolical racism. Only the truly wicked oppose the benefactions of the state! Such clergymen suffer under the most terrible theological delusion of our age, the delusion that substitutes welfare for charity, the state for God, bureaucracy for mercy, and equality for justice. The delusion has such a stranglehold on their thinking that they have no frame of reference to private society. They cannot imagine the evolution of church and private institutions that could guarantee incomes, provide old age comforts, proffer medical help, care for widows and orphans, and heal the emotionally devastated. So the pulpits groan with men who believe that the state has become God or, at least, that the state is godly when run by liberals. When the state is run by a fallen angel of the right, it is up to Congress to protect the kingdom of heaven!

There is, of course, a proper role for the state: one does not discover a doctrine of anarchy in Christianity. It is one thing, however, to rule, to exercise sovereign authority, to defend a people from its enemies, to prevent fraud and violence, and to run courts and achieve justice, and it is quite another thing to transform the state into a mother goddess from whose great breast flows unending milk. To perceive of the state as the Eternal Mother is to become a disciple, priest, and acolyte of government. Liberalism is the priesthood of government. That sort of priesthood should be relegated to political scientists and other strange species and not embraced by the Christian clergy. The Mother Goddess may be voluptuous, but she is not in any sense Christian. Unfortunately, the very sacredness of the Christian Church has been put to the service of politicians and ideologues and bureaucrats. The blessings of the Lord of hosts are invoked on behalf of the tax-and-spend liturgy of Harry Hopkins. The church's sacredness, its transcendence, and its divinity have all been ruthlessly exploited by the disciples of the left.

To reject the state as the fountain of salvation is not in any sense to abandon those in need. The church has its own riches, not all of which are material, and it has a power, not all of which springs from its worldly will. It is through faith that the poor will be cared for and by faith that the church can assist every person who comes to it with any conceivable need. Christianity alone discovers a purpose in suffering; it alone can offer a desperate person a reason to bear his ordeal. Even now, in its evanescent condition, the church could, with faith, found new hospitals; establish new monastic orders that would appeal to the multitudes who are sick of materialism; foster income security programs; underwrite

134

halfway houses for addicts and alcoholics; found new colleges, new seminaries, and new grade and high schools; find jobs and opportunities for the disinherited in the ghettos; rehabilitate criminals, transform prisons into places of hope; found kindergartens and day-care centers for working mothers; and run crisis centers with a Christian orientation that could truly comfort the panicked and the troubled.

It has the resources to do all this now; it lacks only faith and will and correct doctrine. There is little hope in its ability to plunge into such a constructive effort as long as it remains infatuated with the goddess of government. So long as socialism is the veiled goal of so many clergymen, the church will remain paralyzed in many of its congregations and functions. Unquestionably, the church could do more for the innumerable casualties of modern industrial-technological society than even the most benevolent government, because the thing needed most of all is spiritual help, and this is precisely what the state cannot offer. The church can help materially as well. Its brotherhoods and sisterhoods, functioning amid poverty, perform prodigies of work and education at minimal material cost. Church charities are marvels, without the high overhead of government welfare and public education. The state is now discovering that it has reached the point of diminishing returns; if it burdens its citizens any more, it will shrivel the entire economy and decrease total abundance rather than redistribute a rising abundance. A camel's back can carry only so much straw. So the church has an opening, an opportunity to forge ahead before the demagogues take the fatal plunge toward confiscatory taxes. A faithful church, trusting in the power of God, can still rescue American and Western European society from the crushing embrace of socialism, but the time is one minute to midnight.

It is not the business of the church to build utopias on earth. The church is neither a competitor of, nor an alternative to, socialism. Neither is it a rival of government or the welfare state. It is a religion, in the world, but not a part of the world. Its first mission is to defend its prerogatives and freedom and, beyond that, to create a haven, a retreat for all who come to it. Its charity and mercy are not alternatives to welfarism, to be imposed everywhere, but rather are available to those who seek them. The church is a fortress, a refuge from tumultuous, secular, pagan society. It should be able to supply a Christian education for those families that are disgusted with public schools and to operate fine colleges for those who are appalled at the hurly-burly of pot-soaked nihilistic state campuses. It ought to be able to offer a vigorous, ecstatic, and spiritually rewarding monastic life to those whose inner austerity and love of service find no outlet in secular life. It should supply its own homes for the aged and build new orphanages, all totally divorced from the activities of the state. It ought to be able to help the medically indigent who appeal to it and to do more to relieve the loneliness of shut-ins and prisoners.

Thus, it would impose itself on no one, but would always be available to all who are driven to it by the hell of modern mass society and nihilist democracy. It would be a serene haven, a calm harbor for the desperate. It would not be an alternative to government, but rather an excellent moral example. The City of God is not a utopian scheme for this world, and the church cannot pursue gnostic follies without betraying God. Its good works and wonders follow in the wake of its faith. Its saints may teach and convert the world, but the church must always remain aloof from an active politics. The church cannot always avoid plunging into politics, especially when its existence is threatened or its basic moral teachings are besieged, but it cannot attach itself to a party or ideology or place itself at the service of politicians. If Jesus chose not to be a secular king, it is also true that He entered some political disputes, such as the burning question of paying taxes to Rome. The church is not a ruler, lawgiver, divider, or temporal sovereign, but it must sometimes move in the spheres of politics.

One of the things the church could do immediately is to renounce political parties of all sorts. Christians could easily rebuke partisan warfare, which leads to such ugliness as the Watergate affair, by refusing to fund both parties and by refusing to give politicians church forums. Americans give tens of millions of dollars annually to political parties, and all that money tends to increase the stranglehold of the public sector over private life, no matter which party receives it, the Republicans no less than the Democrats. Such money does not so much win elections as escalate the intensity of political strife to Watergate levels, and the more intense that strife, the more politicians are compelled to make foolish promises. In other words, a Christian rebuke of all politics would eventually have a favorable impact on private life. Leftist ideology contributes to massive government, but so does a fierce politics fueled by too much money. If even a modest portion of the money now donated voluntarily to politicians were instead given to church charities, the result would be breathtaking.

I am not suggesting that a Christian rebuke of the parties should take the form of an eternal verity. Rather, it is a remedy for these times. Neither does the renunciation of politics by Christians imply a renunciation of the franchise or a lessening of political awareness. It is always necessary to know who the greater and lesser scoundrels are. Basically, the renunciation is a Christian moral gesture that finds its roots in the Lord's rejection of secular kingship. By dying that death, by surrendering our hope in power, we are freed to plunge into a renewal of the life of the church. So long as the church is not persecuted, the evolution of new religious life within its congregations can proceed quite without reference to the state and its teeming, grubby officeseekers. The church should be a haven, even from politics.

I am not suggesting that the church should become a hostile counterculture at war with the state. Obedience to all governors is a Christian virtue, and it should be done cheerfully and without grudge. I am suggesting, rather, that Christians center their lives in the church and thus automatically rebuild the private life and individual liberty they see being daily eroded by grotesque government. The counterculture ought to be left to the Hippies and their epigoni. It is true that an increasingly secular, socialist, and nihilist society will begin to harass and trouble the church. A haven of peace, serenity, and inequality will be too much for the legions of the left to tolerate, but the church will not and cannot die. It is the only fortress that grows in strength by opening its doors wider. The more troubled the secular world is, the more of its desperate casualties will be driven toward a church with its doors wide open, promising love, joy, and peace to all who enter.

In the future it will be less and less possible to be both a committed leftist and a Christian; indeed, it is possible now only by muddling and obscuring the doctrines of each. To amalgamate the religion with the ideology is to do violence to both. Those who profess to be leftist Christians are even now engaged in a desperate juggling act in which all the balls and bottles must tumble to the ground. The whole New Testament—not mere fragments—decries the secular thrust of leftism. The state can never substitute for the cross. The only possible way to amalgamate the two is to "evolve" Christianity—that is, to rewrite it literally, and that is exactly what "the God is dead" school of theologians is about.

This book has been primarily an exegesis of the New Testament itself, because the scriptures carry the greatest authority. There is a great deal more scripture pointing in the same direction that could not be included within the purview of this volume. In addition, the traditional teachings of the church are available, and they are generally faithful to the Gospels of Matthew, Mark, Luke, and John. I surely do not read leftists out of the church or raise the dark flags of heresy. A commitment to God and an eagerness to love cover a multitude of doctrinal problems. I exclude no one, and content myself merely with pointing out that the chasm daily grows wider between the blueprints of the left-utopians and the teachings of Jesus of Nazareth. Eventually, some people must leap to one side or the other. If He could invite all to follow Him and have faith in Him, it is surely not up to me to drive anyone away.

I anticipate that those who are more firmly committed to leftist and liberal social doctrine than they are to the church will drift away, pursuing their own gods. It is the intent of this book to invite them back and to draw their attention to the doctrinal difficulties they face. Some have drifted very far; they marry homosexuals, advocate trial or experimental marriages, and turn their churches into acid rockfest theaters, while others suppose that presidents are divine. It is for them we must pray.